How the Internet Shapes Collective Actions

DOI: 10.1057/9781137440006.0001

Palgrave Studies in Cyberpsychology

Series Editor: Jens Binder, Nottingham Trent University, UK

Titles include

Sandy Schumann
HOW THE INTERNET SHAPES COLLECTIVE ACTIONS

John Waterworth and Giuseppe Riva
FEELING PRESENT IN THE PHYSICAL WORLD AND COMPUTER-MEDIATED
ENVIRONMENTS

Christian Happ and André Melzer
EMPATHY AND VIOLENT VIDEO GAMES

Palgrave Studies in Cyberpsychology
Series Standing Order ISBN 978-1-137-44948-1 hardback
(*outside North America only*)

You can receive future titles in this series as they are published by placing a standing order. Please contact your bookseller or, in case of difficulty, write to us at the address below with your name and address, the title of the series and the ISBN quoted above.

Customer Services Department, Macmillan Distribution Ltd, Houndmills, Basingstoke, Hampshire RG21 6XS, England

DOI: 10.1057/9781137440006.0001

palgrave▸pivot

How the Internet Shapes Collective Actions

Sandy Schumann

University of Oxford, UK
Wiener-Anspach Foundation, Belgium
Université Libre de Bruxelles, Belgium

palgrave
macmillan

DOI: 10.1057/9781137440006.0001

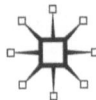

First published 2015 by
PALGRAVE MACMILLAN

Palgrave Macmillan in the UK is an imprint of Macmillan Publishers Limited, registered in England, company number 785998, of Houndmills, Basingstoke, Hampshire, RG21 6XS.

Palgrave Macmillan in the US is a division of St Martin's Press LLC, 175 Fifth Avenue, New York, NY 10010.

Palgrave Macmillan is the global academic imprint of the above companies and has companies and representatives throughout the world.

Palgrave® and Macmillan® are registered trademarks in the United States, the United Kingdom, Europe and other countries.

ISBN: 978–1–137–44001–3 EPUB
ISBN: 978–1–137–44000–6 PDF
ISBN: 978–1–137–43999–4 Hardback

This book is printed on paper suitable for recycling and made from fully managed and sustained forest sources. Logging, pulping and manufacturing processes are expected to conform to the environmental regulations of the country of origin.

A catalogue record for this book is available from the British Library.

A catalog record for this book is available from the Library of Congress.

www.palgrave.com/pivot

DOI: 10.1057/9781137440006

Contents

DOI: 10.1057/9781137440006.0001

DOI: 10.1057/9781137440006.0001

List of Tables

DOI: 10.1057/9781137440006.0002

Acknowledgements

I would like to thank my supervisors and collaborators, Olivier Klein, Karen Douglas, and Anastasia Kavada, for inspiring and encouraging my work in the last four years. In addition, I want to express my gratitude to Greenpeace International for supporting my research. Finally, I thank the funding agency – le Fonds de la Recherche Scientifique Belgium – that granted me an Aspirate fellowship (2010–2014) to conduct my doctoral research and to complete this book.

▶

DOI: 10.1057/9781137440006.0003

Introduction

Abstract: *Ever since it first carried commercial traffic more than 20 years ago, the Internet has been viewed as globe-shifting, revolutionizing even such complex social phenomena as collective actions.* In How the Internet Shapes Collective Actions *I discuss this claim and review current empirical evidence that highlights how Internet-enabled technologies impact individuals' action tendencies. The Introduction sets the tone of the book and illustrates the main questions that are addressed in the following chapters. Moreover, I provide a brief chapter outline highlighting three principal avenues along which the Internet shapes collective actions: a) The Internet fosters self-organized and personalized actions, b) it provides a platform for online engagement, and, finally, c) gathering information or participating in discussions on the Internet incites offline collective actions.*

Schumann, Sandy. *How the Internet Shapes Collective Actions.* Basingstoke: Palgrave Macmillan, 2015. DOI: 10.1057/9781137440006.0004.

"Social media is the worst menace to society" (Letsch, 2013, para. 4), claimed the Turkish Prime Minister Recep Tayyip Erdoğan as a response to weeks of anti-government protests in Turkey in the spring of 2013. Erdoğan condemned social network, (micro) blogging, and content sharing platforms for inciting millions of citizens to join countrywide demonstrations and sit-ins – or, as he stated, for "inciting the public to break the law" (Eissenstat, 2014, para. 7). Twenty-nine Twitter users were arrested and put on trial on these grounds (Gardner, 2014).[1] In 2014, a severe case of corruption by government officials was leaked on Twitter and further protests erupted in Turkey; shortly after, Twitter was blocked for two weeks. As these events unfolded, it remained unclear whether the Turkish authorities took the measures to curtail citizens' rights of freedom of expression or because they considered the Internet (also) as a driving force of the collective actions. Anecdotes from past social movements do lend support to the latter postulation.

On New Year's Day of 1994, the Zapatista Army of National Liberation – a largely Mayan group from the south of Mexico – occupied five cities in the state of Chiapas and declared war on the Mexican government. The uprising for participatory democracy, indigenous freedom, and economic justice was quickly crushed down by government forces, leaving the Zapatistas to retreat into the jungle. Nevertheless, in the last 20 years, the Zapatistas attained political and economic autonomy in five regions of Chiapas and inspired actions in solidarity with the alter-globalization and anti-neoliberal movement in Mexico and abroad (Ronfeldt, Arquilla, Fuller, & Fuller, 1998). One factor that may have contributed to their persistence is that – at a time when the Internet and tools for computer-mediated communication (CMC) were still in its infancy – the Zapatistas advocated their cause in an innovative, a digital manner. The activists used email lists and usenet groups to spread their message to the media and civil society around the world. Above all, the Internet-enabled technologies provided effective tools to receive specialist advice, encouragement, and funding from an international support network.

It only became evident with time how tremendously helpful the Internet had been to advance the Zapatista movement. However, when millions of people took to the streets all around the Arab world in the spring of 2011, the protests were quickly labelled a Facebook or Twitter revolution, suggesting that social media had had a considerable influence on the diffusion and rapid growth of the uprisings (Morozov, 2011). Although the dissident sentiments in, for example, Tunisia or

DOI: 10.1057/9781137440006.0004

Egypt would "have bubbled over even without the web" (Krotoski, 2013, p. 146), it must be acknowledged that the participatory Internet formed an important platform to coordinate protests and to communicate with fellow citizens.

More precisely, social network, (micro) blogging, and content sharing platforms, on which information about demonstrations was posted along with images of cats and holiday pictures, functioned as an information broker. Testimonials and reports of marches, attacks, or victories were recorded with mobile devices and uploaded to the Internet, informing a global audience while bypassing official media censorship. Almost half of the demonstrators who had attended the first protest on Tahrir Square in Cairo on 25 January 2011 indicated in an interview study that they had shared images or videos of the events online (Tufekci & Wilson, 2012). Activists received through the same channels endorsing messages from a global community of supporters, which may have stimulated further engagement (Skinner, 2011).

Although the exact impact is difficult to quantify, the Zapatista Movement and the Arab Spring illustrate vividly that the Internet can be an important tool for citizens and civil society to pursue social change through protests or sit-ins, volunteering, making donations, and signing petitions, that is, through collective actions that are taken by a "large number of people who experience a common problem or issue and seek common solutions" (Bennett & Segerberg, 2013, p. 1). A survey by the Pew Research Center Internet & American Life Project suggested that members of civic, social, and religious groups believe that the Internet helps raise awareness about the issues that are important for their group; 38 per cent of the respondents confirmed that the Internet could play a major role in solving societal problems (Rainie, Purcell, & Smith, 2011). This optimistic point of view, however, has been challenged ever since the Internet gained popularity in the early 1990s. Scholars criticized that Internet-enabled technologies undermine meaningful civic or political actions, because people would become "lonely bowlers" who prefer to be entertained online rather than get engaged for their community (Putnam, 1995; time displacement hypothesis).

The HomeNet field trial was one of the first studies (i.e., conducted between 1995 and 1997) to examine the social effects of the Internet (Kraut et al., 1998). The researchers offered Internet access to 93 families from the Pittsburgh area (USA) and showed that more Internet use – the average hours spent online per week – was related to reduced social

DOI: 10.1057/9781137440006.0004

involvement as well as to decreased psychological well-being (Kraut et al., 1998). A follow-up longitudinal study between 1998 and 1999 did not support these findings; on the contrary, the authors highlighted that Internet use enhanced the size of participants' social circles and their community involvement. Especially extroverts benefited from the Internet and "its opportunities to enhance (...) everyday social lives" (Kraut, Kiesler, Boneva, Cummings, & Helgeson, 2002, p. 69).

Recently, and somewhat building on Putnam's time displacement hypothesis (1995), it has been red-flagged that the ubiquity of social media platforms may entail hidden costs for groups that want to attain a collective purpose. Convenient and easy-to-access online services are thought to encourage so-called slacker-activism – slacktivism – that is, low-cost and low-risk online collective actions such as signing online petitions or "liking" a group's Facebook page. The latter could foreclose enduring participation in collective actions; as users satisfy their need to take action through simple clicks they should be less willing to join subsequent protests or sit-ins (Morozov, 2009).

To illustrate this argument, consider the KONY 2012 campaign: The American non-profit organization Invisible Children published in March 2012 a video on YouTube in which they presented their work that (allegedly) supports African communities in the fight against the Ugandan war lord Joseph Kony and its Lord's Resistance Army. The organization refers to the video as an experiment that was carried out to see whether "an online video [can] make an obscure war criminal famous? And if he was famous, would the world work together to stop him?" (Invisible Children, 2014). More than 98 million people had watched the video on YouTube by October 2013; 3.7 million users pledged their support to Invisible Children by signing so-called pledge cards online (Invisible Children, 2014). Overall, it seems as if KONY 2012 was a (digital) success. But when Invisible Children issued an international call for their Cover the Night campaign – during which posters of the "wanted" Joseph Kony were to be put up in cities around the globe – barely anyone participated (Carroll, 2012).

It goes beyond the scope of this book to discuss the controversies of the KONY 2012 campaign and the organization Invisible Children (see Zuckerman, 2012, for a discussion). The discrepancy between the overwhelming virtual attention and the limited support offline, however, sparked a lively debate, questioning whether the Internet can truly foster committed engagement or whether it promotes low-threshold activism

DOI: 10.1057/9781137440006.0004

by users who do not want "to get their hands dirty" (Christensen, 2011, para. 28). A fundraising campaign of UNICEF Sweden expressed these concerns more explicitly. The Unicef Sweden Director of Communications – Petra Hallebrant – explained that "We like likes, and social media could be a good first step to get involved, but it cannot stop there (....) Likes don't save children's lives" (Khazan, 2013, para. 5).

Scope of the book

At the time of writing, 40 per cent of the world population has Internet access – a staggering 40-fold increase since 1995 (Internet Live Stats, 2014a). In countries such as Germany, the United Kingdom, and Canada, Internet penetration reached more than 80 per cent in 2011 (Graham & De Sabbata, 2013). And in the 28 member states of the European Union, 56 per cent of the population uses the Internet on a daily basis (Eurostat, 2014). As manifold social media platforms, services for computer-mediated communication, and more than one billion websites (Internet Live Stats, 2014b) are becoming an essential part of the life of people around the globe, the Internet could have an unprecedented impact on citizens' collective action tendencies and the overall course of social movements. But how exactly does the Internet shape collective actions?

The participatory Internet, for instance, decentralizes the flow of information and impacts thereby the power relations between decision-making entities and (ordinary) citizens. Are collective actions that rely on social media to inform and mobilize supporters thus more inclusive and self-organized, driven by loose networks rather than formal groups? And could Internet-enabled technologies even influence specific mobilizing processes to enhance the scale of collective actions? That is, can Internet use, for example, strengthen identification with a group, increase campaign knowledge, or reduce the costs of engagement and hence prompt collective actions? If so, do Internet services and social media platforms serve as tools to stimulate participation of previously unengaged citizens? Or is the Internet simply reinforcing activities of experienced supporters? Finally, what digital practices do cause-related, advocacy, and social movement organizations prefer to coordinate and encourage stakeholders? In other words, does the Internet – in practice – really play a role for collective actions?

DOI: 10.1057/9781137440006.0004

In *How the Internet Shapes Collective Actions* I respond to these questions, providing a broad overview of the academic literature as well as insights from popular science, practitioners, and activists. I will *not* introduce a universal theoretical framework to explain the effects of the Internet on collective actions or present case studies of past social movements. Instead, I will draw on an ever-expanding body of empirical research – some being well-established, some requiring further inquiry – from disciplines such as social psychology, communication, and political science. I will discuss work that examined one particular or diverse digital platforms and Internet services, studies that assessed specific events or general processes, experimental analyses, and ethnographic research.

The book offers a comprehensive introduction for students and scholars who want to explore the mobilizing potential of Internet-enabled technologies, their complex influence on collective actions and related social phenomena. Moreover, *How the Internet Shapes Collective Actions* is a resource for activists and practitioners. I will recap how cause-related, advocacy, and social movement organizations use the Internet to promote campaigns. Further, I identify stakeholders' preferred digital practices to learn about, interact with, or get engaged for a group online, indicating strategies to best harness supporters' need for involvement.

Throughout the book, I will mention many examples of social media and features of the participatory Internet that encourage users to generate and disseminate content – including social network, (micro) blogging, video and photo sharing sites as well as blogs, wikis, and podcasts. However, not only the collaborative use of the Internet can shape collective actions. In fact, I will demonstrate that gathering information online – often viewed as characteristic of the web 1.0^2 – is a key predictor of collective actions. In addition, to date, cause-related, advocacy, and social movement organizations are (still) primarily using their web presence to disseminate information (Lovejoy & Saxton, 2012; Guo & Saxton, 2014).

At this point, I want to issue a warning: I do not suggest that the Internet – the medium – brings about demonstrations, support for electoral campaigns, volunteering, and ultimately social change. This technology-deterministic perspective that concludes "Tweets were sent. Dictators were toppled. Internet = democracy. QED." (para. 1) is too restrictive (Morozov, 2011); it ignores complex intra-personal and intra-group dynamics that interact with or underlie individuals' online behaviour and that qualify whether and how Internet use relates to

DOI: 10.1057/9781137440006.0004

collective actions. Rather, citizens' *use of* Internet-enabled technologies keeps collective actions "alive and connected" (González-Bailón, Borge-Holthoefer, & Moreno, 2013), it amplifies the social phenomena or processes that evoke engagement (see Van Dijk, 2012). During the uprisings in Cairo in 2011, it was not simply because of Facebook that tens of thousands of people stood up for democracy on Tahrir square. However, those who sympathized with the dissent sentiments frequently learnt via Facebook about the possibility to express their opinions and to strive for political alternatives by attending the protests. In many cases this information might have been accessed more quickly on the Internet than if citizens had relied on face-to-face communication. As a consequence, more people were mobilized much faster. In other words, the intense use of social media platforms did not change but rather reinforced existing avenues of mobilization.

Taking a snapshot of the current insights on *How the Internet Shapes Collective Actions* may seem like an exercise with mainly practical relevance, driven by the need to understand how information technology stimulates actions and possibly offering an explanation for social movements that emerged in recent years. Nevertheless, the inquiry also makes an important theoretical contribution. Because at the centre of this analysis rests an additional question: Can a medium that is accused of fostering individuality and isolation encourage actions on behalf of others, for a collective purpose (Brunsting & Postmes, 2002)? The answer is yes; I will highlight how groups can be formed and collective identities be developed with the help of Internet-enabled technologies. After all, the social aspect of the Internet is not only a matter of generating and sharing content. The social aspect of the Internet also entails that supporters of a common cause – citizens who are united in a struggle or who agree on wanting to end the struggles of others – build and strengthen relationships, despite the fact that they are all sitting alone in front of a computer.

Chapter structure

In essence, I propose in the following five chapters three avenues along which the Internet can shape collective actions. First, the participatory Internet fosters self-organized forms of engagement, impacting the nature of collective actions. Second, distinct types of Internet

DOI: 10.1057/9781137440006.0004

use – information retrieval and discussions – incite *offline* participation and therefore enhance the scale of collective actions. Third, the Internet diversifies individuals' action repertoires by offering a platform for Internet-based collective actions.

As a starting point, I will review in Chapter 1 two common conceptualizations of collective actions – as applied in social psychological research and proposed by Olson in his seminal work *The Logic of Collective Action* (1968) – that emphasize that formal groups drive collective actions by providing incentives, setting agendas, and structuring individuals' affiliation. Shifting patterns of Internet use as well as recent social movements suggest that this strictly organization-brokered understanding of collective actions should be reconsidered. More precisely, the participatory Internet enables a decentralized, horizontal coordination of collective actions and promotes *connective* actions. The interactive features of social media platforms allow users to spread information through personal networks, to get in touch with like-minded citizens, and provide even means to act on personal action frames online (Bennett & Segerberg, 2012).

In Chapter 2, I will discuss specific mobilizing processes and review research that examined how digital practices affect participation in *offline* collective actions. The most common type of Internet use is targeted information access. I will explore how gathering real-time updates from collective actions, practical information, insights about grass-root organizations, and political news online facilitates, for instance, voting, volunteering, protesting, or making donations (Bimber, 2003; Boulianne, 2009). The effects will be explained from an intra-personal or intra-group perspective. Easy and quick access to diverse information reduces the costs of engagement; information can also be empowering and increase knowledge or interest in current affairs and community matters, ultimately enhancing the willingness to take actions. Alternatively, sharing information about their activities, achievements, and norms helps define the collective identity of a group and sets an agenda that supporters may refer to when they get engaged (Postmes, Spears, Lee, & Nowak, 2005).

Previous research highlighted further that information that is acquired on the Internet promotes online and offline political discussions and therefore encourages individuals to display, for instance, a banner, donate to an activist organization, or join a protest and rally (Nah, Veenstra, & Sha, 2006). In online deliberations dispersed users who are concerned about the same cause can be united to establish a

DOI: 10.1057/9781137440006.0004

common group identity in a bottom-up process (Postmes, Spears, et al., 2005). The interactions may further foster supporters' identification with a group and enhance the politicization of collective identities – individuals can arrive more quickly at the conclusion that they share grievances and third parties or society as a whole can more easily be included in a campaign (Alberici & Milesi, 2013). Consequentially, gathering information and participating in dialogues on the Internet can enhance the scale of collective actions.

Beyond mobilizing offline collective actions, the Internet also provides an infrastructure for digital engagement, diversifying individuals' action repertoires, and promoting activities that are independent of time, space, or the physical co-presence of fellow supporters (Theocharis, Lowe, Van Deth, & García Albacete, 2013). In Chapter 3, I explore Internet-based collective actions – for instance, online petitions and donations – that are available to everyone with Internet access and that pose low risks. These low-threshold online collective actions (Van Laer & Van Aelst, 2010) drastically reduce the barriers for participation. But, as advocates of the slacktivism critique have argued, this convenience may have a down side: Quick clicks and "likes" could make users feel good about themselves, increase their self-esteem, or satisfy the need to take action and therefore foreclose enduring participation (Christensen, 2011; Gladwell, 2010; Morozov, 2009).

The slacktivism hypothesis is passionately debated by scholars and practitioners; its central substitute proposition, however, has not yet been systematically investigated. To address this gap in the literature, I will present a line of my own experimental research. Based on three studies, I conclude that low-cost and low-risk Internet-based collective actions can indeed demobilize, because supporters believe they contributed sufficiently to their group's success. In fact, low-threshold online collective actions and – possibly more involving – offline engagement are considered as equally valid and potent (Freelon, 2014; Tufekci & Freelon, 2013).

In Chapter 4, I will consider the aforementioned insights of academic research in a practical context and illustrate how cause-related, advocacy, and social movement organizations use the Internet to raise awareness, attract funds, or interact with stakeholders (Briones, Kuch, Liu, & Jin, 2011; Lovejoy & Saxton, 2012). Importantly, I will not review handbooks that suggest how groups *should* employ the Internet. Rather, I will put forward analyses of groups' or activists' online activities. It is evident that

DOI: 10.1057/9781137440006.0004

grass-root organizations are not yet taking full advantage of the freely available and easy-to-handle tools of the participatory Internet. For instance, interactions between representatives of an organization and its stakeholders are less common than top-down information dissemination; connections amongst supporters are very seldom encouraged. This pattern is partially in line with the expectations of citizens who use the Internet to get engaged on behalf of a cause: I will report findings from my own research that suggest that supporters of an environmental advocacy group considered gathering news and information on the Internet as the most influential online behaviour to contribute to their group's goals.

In the final chapter, Chapter 5, I will summarize once more all arguments and highlight challenges of previous research. For instance, to date, it has not yet been established whether digital practices can actually influence concrete initiatives or policy making processes. Especially low-cost and low-risk online collective actions have been criticized for having no social impact (Gladwell, 2010). At the same time, there is no empirical evidence available to support or contest this postulation. Further, the (potential) mobilizing potential of the Internet is restricted in the sense that large segments of society still do not have access to the Internet or do not have the skills to use information technology.

Bringing the book to a close, I will take a closer look at two important – technological and social – developments that may affect how the Internet shapes collective actions in the future. Responding to increased digital surveillance and sophisticated measures to trace online behaviour, it could be speculated that citizens are increasingly inclined to navigate the Internet in partial or full anonymity. Google announced in July 2014 that users no longer had to register with their full name for its services; The Tor Project aims to offer a way to surf the Internet without leaving digital footprints. As individuals take advantage of these opportunities, are, for instance, dynamics of community building affected? Is it more difficult to define group identities – and thereby steer collective actions – through online discussions?

Finally, I will raise the topic of algorithmic filtering, that is, algorithms of social media platforms or websites control which information is likely to be viewed. Drawing on recent protests in Ferguson (USA) – evoked by the killing of the unarmed black teenager Michael Brown by a police officer – I will recap how news about the incident and the subsequent

DOI: 10.1057/9781137440006.0004

demonstrations was more visible on some social media platforms than on others. I will conclude the discourse by referring to Tufekci (2014a) and Zuckerman (2014) who highlighted that algorithmic censorship – suppressing certain information online – can determine public discourse and thereby shape civic and political engagement. Because "what happens to #Ferguson [on Twitter] affects what happens to Ferguson" (Tufekci, 2014a, para. 36).

Notes

1 In September 2014, 28 citizens were acquitted and one person was convicted for defamation.
2 The participatory Internet and social media are often referred to as the web 2.0. Compared to the web 1.0, the web 2.0 is not a different technology – the Internet afforded "technically" since its early days that users interact and share content. The web 2.0 signifies a shift in Internet use patterns, from information retrieval to the active production and co-creation of content (Kavada, 2012).

DOI: 10.1057/9781137440006.0004

1

How the Internet Promotes Self-organized Collective Actions

Abstract: *Research on collective actions, its underpinnings and dynamics, flourished in the last decades and stimulated contributions from a multitude of disciplines. I commence Chapter 1 by introducing two common conceptualizations of collective actions that emphasize the relevance of a formal group to coordinate and structure collective actions. Following Bennett and Segerberg (2012), the participatory Internet promotes – rather than organization-brokered collective actions – self-organized engagement. More precisely, the Internet allows individuals to access information to develop personal action frames, fostering collective actions that are driven by unique aspirations and not group agendas. In addition, social media platforms may take on the role of cause-related, advocacy, and movement organizations, affording connections and communication between supporters.*

Schumann, Sandy. *How the Internet Shapes Collective Actions*. Basingstoke: Palgrave Macmillan, 2015.
DOI: 10.1057/9781137440006.0005.

Throughout the past centuries, social uprisings, protests, and strikes have been an important catalyst for societal and political developments, enabling individuals to express their criticism of social systems, governments, or ideologies and bringing about social change (Melucci, 1996). Research that assesses the underpinnings and dynamics of such collective actions has flourished since the 1960s; it includes contributions from economics, sociology, political science, anthropology, history, and social psychology. Anthropological studies investigated, for instance, the cultural symbols that are produced in the course of collective actions. Research in political science examined collective actions as political actors as well as the role of political opportunities; long-term developments of actions and accounts of the events that preceded them were, for example, explored in historical research (Roggenband & Klandermans, 2010).

The diverse disciplinary roots of collective action research implicate a multitude of definitions and theoretical frameworks. It is impossible to capture all perspectives in this book, and interested readers are advised to see Klandermans and Roggeband's *Handbook of Social Movements Across Disciplines* (2010) for a comprehensive overview. In the following, I will introduce two conceptualizations of collective actions that are grounded in social psychological research and Olson's (1968) *Logic of Collective Action*. The approaches emphasize that individuals participate in collective actions on behalf of formal groups that steer demonstrations or sit-ins. In the second part of the chapter, I present the work of Bennett and Segerberg (2012, 2013) who propose that the Internet influences this group-centred understanding of collective actions by shifting power relations between decision-making entities and citizens. More precisely, the authors suggest that the participatory Internet encourages self-organized collective actions – connective actions. Rather than cause-related, advocacy, or social movement organizations, social media platforms enable communication as well as the coordination of collective actions.

Towards a definition of collective actions

On the broadest level, the various definitions of collective actions that have been put forward can be distinguished into a micro- and macro-level perspective. The latter considers – amongst others – a country's

DOI: 10.1057/9781137440006.0005

position in the world economy and structural changes such as globalization that may altogether create a political, social, and cultural context in which collective actions are more or less likely, in which, for instance, resources or opportunities to take action are more or less available. Further, the nation state and governing bodies may grant possibilities and set limits for collective actions (Smith & Fetner, 2010). Pertaining to the central question of this book – How does the Internet shape collective actions? – technological advancements, such as the introduction of broadband Internet, are as well macro-level forces that could affect action tendencies.

That being said, I will apply in the following chapters a micro-level approach to collective actions and take the individual as the unit of analysis. Such an actor-oriented angle explores individuals' thoughts, feelings, and behaviour (intentions), but does not imply that collective actions are taken by only one person. More precisely, the work that I will present most commonly investigates whether Internet use – the average time spent online – or specific digital practices – accessing information or entertainment – shape individuals' willingness and actual attendance in collective actions. Macro-level influences such as the political environment or legislation certainly impact these relations; they are, however, rarely explicitly considered in the analyses.

Group-brokered collective actions

Collective actions include a wide range of activities; they may be set in public, such as demonstrations and sit-ins, or happen in private, such as making a donation and boycotting a product. Certain collective actions require particular skills, such as lobbying or hacking websites; others can be taken by anyone who is interested in supporting a campaign by wearing, for instance, a button or by signing a petition. In social psychological research, the aforementioned examples are referred to as collective actions *if* they are performed by members of low-status groups to improve the position, power, and influence of the entire disadvantaged group (Wright, Taylor, & Moghaddam, 1990). For example, migrant workers who protest to advocate labour rights for all migrant workers engage in a collective action.

Further, high-status group members may join collective actions to maintain the status-quo and the oppression of disadvantaged groups

DOI: 10.1057/9781137440006.0005

(Van Zomeren & Iyer, 2009). Following the previous example, if members of the host society start a petition to prevent migrant workers from attaining labour rights so that all members of the host society do not have to pay more for migrants' work, this campaign is understood as a collective action. Alternatively, members of the host society who join the demonstration of migrant workers take a collective action in solidarity with the low-status group. Finally, opinion-based groups – two or more individuals who agree on an opinion and for whom sharing this point of view determines their group membership (Bliuc, McGarty, Reynolds, & Muntele, 2007) – initiate collective actions to promote their ideas. A sit-in around a tree that ought to be cut down can be viewed as a collective action of an environmental group, if the protesters agree on the fact that protecting biodiversity is crucial and if they want to advance this mission through their action.

To address these four scenarios, Postmes and Brunsting (2002) referred to collective actions as "actions undertaken by individuals or groups for a collective purpose, such as the advancement of a particular ideology or idea, or the political struggles with another group" (pp. 290–291). If citizens, however, attend protests or make donations with the goal to gain personal benefits, the actions are not considered collective but *personal* actions (Wright et al., 1990). Concluding, collective actions are conditional on individuals' affiliation with a group that they act for or on behalf of. This approach resonates with work that examines patterns of civic engagement. Gil de Zúñiga and Valenzuela (2011) describe civic engagement as a voluntary civic activity that is concerned with social and/or community issues that aims to ensure collective goals and well-being. Examples for civic engagement include volunteering for a group that plans to build a play ground in the neighbourhood or hosting community meetings to promote the expansion of a natural reserve. In other words, through civic engagement citizens strive to achieve a collective purpose that benefits a larger group that one is part of or sympathizes with.

At this point, I want to highlight why such a sense of group membership, a sense of belonging, is a relevant constituent of (taking) collective actions. Self-categorization theory (Turner, Hogg, Oakes, Reicher, & Wetherell, 1987) postulates that individuals' self-concept – their answers to the question "Who am I?" – consists of a collection of cognitive representations that include distinct, personal characteristics – I have brown eyes, I am a curious person, I like to sleep in – as well as references to

DOI: 10.1057/9781137440006.0005

group memberships – I belong to my local volleyball club, I am a member of the classical music society, I am Swedish. These representations are organized in a hierarchical system on different levels of abstraction. At the subordinate, the interpersonal level, idiosyncratic characteristics define the self-concept; the personal identity is salient (Turner, 1999). On the intermediate, the intergroup level social identities[1] are salient. The latter represent the cognitive aspect of being a member of a certain group, knowing that one belongs to a group, as well as the associated "emotional and value significance" (Tajfel, 1972, p. 31). All individual and group differences deem, however, unimportant on the superordinate, the interspecies level of self-categorization where individuals define themselves and others as part of the all encompassing category human beings (Turner, 1999).

Participation in collective actions, as discussed thus far, relies on self-categorization at an intergroup level. Then, group norms govern members' perceptions, judgments, attitudes, emotions, and actions, and individual behaviour shifts to collective behaviour (Castano, Yzerbyt, Paladino, & Sacchi, 2002). Consequently, engagement in collective actions is strictly defined by the interpretations and possible sanctions of a group; there is little room to negotiate personalized perspectives. After all, if individuals affiliate with a group they value – in themselves and others – attitudes and behaviour that advance their group's endeavours (Tropp & Brown, 2004).

Mancur Olson (1968) proposes in the *Logic of Collective Action* that groups cannot only rely on members' sense of affiliation, but must introduce as well procedures and incentives to encourage collective actions. Olson (1968) defined collective actions as behaviour that creates a public good, such as a public radio station, a park, or the right for abortion. A public good is non-excludable; it is accessible to all citizens and can also be enjoyed by those who did not fight for its provision. Being rational actors, individuals are thought to consider the costs and benefits of engagement and are likely concluding that *not* participating in collective actions is the most effective choice: The public good can be attained without exerting any effort. This free-riding tendency should be reduced in small groups; here, incentives to foster engagement are administered more easily and individuals should view their contributions as more potent.

To assert the group-brokered nature of the aforementioned conceptualizations of collective actions, consider this example: A demonstration

DOI: 10.1057/9781137440006.0005

is organized by an environmental advocacy group. To become a member, citizens need to register officially with a local representation of the group and pay an annual fee. When the group plans the demonstration, roles are assigned and a structure is established. Some supporters may be responsible for painting signs and banners; others ensure that the demonstration is in line with the city's regulations or arrange transportation. The group leaders prescribe the rationale for the action – for instance, a natural reserve must be established because breeding grounds for birds are disappearing – and members are expected to follow these interpretations. Information about the whereabouts and schedule of the demonstration is spread amongst members; citizens who are not formally affiliated with the group are probably not aware of the action. Importantly, members know that if they want to support their group, they join the demonstration – they would not initiate another action with another goal. Attending the protest will be rewarded with validation from the group leaders and positive feedback from other supporters.

Crowd-enabled collective actions

Now imagine a demonstration where citizens do not know each other; they join for various reasons and learnt about the time and place of the protest though their personal social network rather than a formal group. Bennett and Segerberg (2012, 2013) propose that the ubiquity of the participatory Internet encourages the rise of such self-organized collective actions – *connective* actions – that do not compromise personal beliefs for group ideologies. In other words, social media platforms and its interactive tools may shape the nature of collective actions by shifting the focus from centralized, group-driven engagement to personalized participation.

Users are increasingly generating and disseminating content online, and patterns of news consumption suggest that citizens prefer to receive information that is not filtered by traditional gatekeepers to compile and interpret the material independently (Smith & Rainie, 2010). These developments alter the power relations between decision-making entities such as cause-related, advocacy, and movement organizations and their supporters. Groups are less dominant in setting the tone of a discourse and in steering individuals' points of view. Rather, as Bennett and Segerberg (2013) point out, political and social issues are considered as frames that are adaptable depending on individual needs and concerns.

DOI: 10.1057/9781137440006.0005

As a result, personal action frames – addressing unique aspirations and motivations – are established and collective actions emerge as "an expression of personal hopes, lifestyles, and grievances" (Bennett & Segerberg, 2012, p. 743) – not based on the agendas and incentives of formal groups. Citizens choose tactics from their own and not necessarily organizational repertoires of contention; they are proactive and initiate collective actions online or offline.

Despite this personalization, connective actions do not lack a mission or resolve in chaos. The participatory Internet is a context that is rich in information and that promotes communication: Relationships emerge between users and provide structure, processes, and resources (see also Bimber, Flanagin, & Stohl, 2012; Flanagin, Stohl, & Bimber, 2006). In fact, it has been argued that social media platforms take on the role of cause-related, advocacy, and movement organizations and offer the central tools to coordinate actions. As Gónzalez-Bailón and colleagues (2013) noted, "in the case of recent protests [in North Africa, Spain, Greece, or the United States], large numbers of people were recruited and mobilized in a decentralized, horizontal way, using preexisting networks of communication that were not necessarily (...) political" (p. 947). On Facebook, for instance, users can easily connect with others who are concerned about the same issue by joining Facebook pages – sometimes only temporarily. Organizations can unite on the social network site with other initiatives that address similar missions. In bringing together diverse individuals and causes – being not limited by time, borders, or physical space – such self-organized, loose action networks have a variety of resources available to initiate, coordinate, and stage collective actions. As the number of digital ties grows, information and mobilizing messages spread farther.

More precisely, the participatory Internet enables citizens to report and promote engagement to their personal social network. Thereby calls for actions reach individuals who never would have attended a protest or sit-in – either because they would not want to commit to a fixed organizational agenda or because they would not have been targeted by the mobilizing efforts of formal groups. Ultimately, collective actions become more inclusive. Bennett and Segerberg (2013) hence propose to conceptualize collective actions as actions that are taken by a "large number of people who experience a common problem or issue and seek common solutions" (p. 1). Individuals do not necessarily need to get engaged on behalf of a group, and they may have diverse motives for participation. While research in social psychology emphasizes that actions that are driven by personal benefits are not considered collective actions, Bennett and Segerberg's (2013) working definition is more flexible and acknowledges all possible action frames.

Analyses of 57 demonstrations, which took place in seven European countries between 2009 and 2011, indicated that using online social network sites instead of formal organizations to promote collective actions encouraged indeed more diverse interpretations of the issues that were addressed in the protests. Participants of the connective actions were less embedded in and identified less with a formal group (Cristancho & Anduiza, 2013). The authors further highlighted that previously uninvolved individuals were more likely to join digitally enabled actions as compared to group-brokered demonstrations. Taking a closer look at the 15M protest in Spain in 2011 – calling for social justice, participation, and transparency – the characteristics of crowd-enabled actions were as well supported (Anduiza, Cristancho, & Sabucedo, 2014). No parties or unions were involved in the coordination of the protest, and it received little coverage in print and news media beforehand. Clear leadership roles were not established; around 400 small organizations – of which only 13 per cent had formal membership procedures – were united on the online platform Democracia Real Ya to stage the action. Compared to eight other demonstrations in Spain in 2010 and 2011, more than half of the participants of the 15M protest had heard about it through alternative online media, and 49 per cent had received information about the protest through their personal social network. Protesters were younger, more likely to be female, and unemployed – they represented those who are traditionally less engaged in collective actions.

A final example of a connective action are the Gezi Park protests that took place in 2013 and spread from Istanbul all around Turkey. The protest began on 28 May 2013 as a small action against an urban development plan for Istanbul's Taksim Gezi Park, acceding to which several hundred-years-old trees would have been cut down. The initial sit-in in the park developed a few days later into a camp and attracted thousands of supporters who stayed overnight; a library, medical centre, food distribution, and media channels were established. The protest site soon moved from Gezi Park – it was cleared on 15 June 2013 – to other parks, squares, and the streets all around Turkey. Government authorities reacted to the uprisings with extreme measures, and the police used excessive force, tear gas, and water cannons against the protesters. Although the actions

DOI: 10.1057/9781137440006.0005

were sparked by environmental concerns, they addressed later primarily citizens' concerns about the freedom of the Turkish press, the freedom of expression and assembly, and Prime Minister Erdoğan's politics to construct a new, less secular Turkey. Approximately 3.5 million people attended around 5000 demonstrations.

Again, unlike in a group-brokered collective action, no formal, centralized leadership structures emerged during the Gezi protests. A small assembly had organized the first protests, but in the course of the events no explicit organizing entity was set up. Protesters came from all walks of life, were supporters of different political ideologies, "young and old people, students and bureaucrats, feminists and housewives, Muslims and leftists, Kurds and Alevis, Kemalists and communists, Fenerbahçe and Beşiktaş supporters" (Göle, 2013, para. 27). As Göle stated, "the square [became] (...) a venue or a means for coming together, debating, showing solidarity and intermingling with each other" (2013, para. 34).

Much of the traditional media in Turkey is in hands of the government. In many instances, Turkish newspapers and television did not report about the protests or presented only a particular angle – CNN Turk, for example, showed a penguin documentary when events peaked to highest tension and tear gas was fired in Istanbul. As people recognized that television and newspaper are not reliable sources, social media platforms became a central information broker. Without one particular organization taking a leading role, social network, (micro) blogging, and content sharing platforms became the place where real-time information was exchanged, allowing precise responses by the protesters. Twitter was a powerful and instant means to stay updated about what was happening on the ground; citizens and civil society used the platform to communicate and coordinate actions as they evolved. On Facebook, for instance, activists and residents of Istanbul shared where exactly the police was stationed. Amnesty International tweeted phone numbers of lawyers who would assist arrested citizens, and hotels or restaurants close to the protest sites offered demonstrators via social media platforms shelter and food (Hutchinson, 2013).

Take home message

The Internet can shape group-brokered collective actions by encouraging self-organized engagement. Social network, (micro) blogging, and

DOI: 10.1057/9781137440006.0005

content sharing platforms enable users to connect with like-minded citizens, to discuss and coordinate collective actions. Importantly, decentralized and personalized connective actions are not isolating individuals from a collective purpose. On the contrary, crowd-enabled actions address as well a collective struggle and aim to find a collective solution. The pathways of mobilization, motives for participation, and the repertoires of contention, however, are not defined by a formal group but driven by unique aspirations and personal networks.

Note

1 Self-categorization theory was developed based on identity theory (Tajfel & Turner, 1979). In the latter, however, personal and social identity are defined as the extreme poles of a continuum of self-concept rather than levels of abstraction; an individual's position is affected by the perceived permeability of group boundaries, the ease to leave the group, and social change belief (for a discussion on the two approaches see Turner, 1999).

DOI: 10.1057/9781137440006.0005

2

How Internet Use Incites Offline Collective Actions

Abstract: *Targeted information retrieval is the most popular type of Internet use. In this chapter I will report research that demonstrated that acquiring information online – political news, real-time information from collective actions, practical information about events, or information about a group's mission and norms – incites participation in collective actions that take place offline. I will discuss the potential underlying processes of these effects, distinguishing an intrapersonal and an intragroup perspective. Moreover, information that is gathered online can foster offline collective actions by promoting online discussions. I will refer to the impact of weak tie connections and highlight three group-level processes that are likely to be shaped by online interactions. That is, group identities may emerge, identification with these groups might be enhanced, and group identities can be politicized.*

Schumann, Sandy. *How the Internet Shapes Collective Actions.* Basingstoke: Palgrave Macmillan, 2015.
DOI: 10.1057/9781137440006.0006.

DOI: 10.1057/9781137440006.0006

What motivates individuals to join protests, boycott products, volunteer, and make donations for a collective purpose? While social scientists identified multiple predictors for collective actions,[1] the avenues for mobilization have become increasingly complex since Sir Tim Berners-Lee launched the World Wide Web on Christmas Day of 1990. Repeatedly, the Internet has been referred to as a means to "galvanise, coordinate, collaborate and overthrow" (Krotoski, 2013, p. 145), as a means to incite, for instance, demonstrations, donations to electoral campaigns, or volunteering (Van Laer & Van Aelst, 2010). Early empirical evidence, however, suggested the opposite: When considering the average time individuals spent online, frequent Internet use reduced individuals' social involvement (Kraut et al., 1998). This sobering message confirmed Robert Putnam's (1995) proposition of a time displacement effect: Finding manifold entertainment online, citizens no longer have the time or the interest to be involved in their community, sports, or religious groups.

As mentioned, Kraut and colleagues (1998; see also Kraut et al., 2002) assessed the hours that participants were online each week – the authors did not consider whether citizens read news, played games, or sent emails. Subsequent studies addressed this issue. More precisely, scholars explored specific Internet use patterns and the relations with *offline* collective actions. The latter work follows the uses and gratification approach, which postulates that individuals actively seek different media and use it in a particular way[2] to fulfil needs, such as the need for diversion and entertainment, the need to construct an identity and to establish social relationships, or the need to have access to information (see Döring, 2010; Katz, Blumler, & Gurevitch, 1974). Consequently, it is "not the media per se that can affect individuals' participation, but [how] (...) individuals use [it]" (Gil de Zúñiga & Valenzuela, 2011, p. 5). Previous research demonstrated that retrieving information on the Internet as well as interacting with fellow users fosters participation in offline collective actions; using the Internet for diversion (e.g., playing games or watching videos) was negatively related to engagement (see Valenzuela, Arriagada, & Scherman, 2012).[3]

In this chapter, I will discuss these findings in more detail and point out how the Internet facilitates informed collective actions across different social and political contexts. More precisely, I will analyse the impact of four classes of information. I will elaborate on the influence of real-time updates from collective actions, on the role of practical information that helps supporters organize their participation as well as on the effect of acquiring political news online. Further, I will review the consequences of disseminating information about the goals, achievements, or ideologies of cause-related, advocacy, and movement organizations. Distinguishing an intrapersonal path – driven by empowerment, reduced costs, and increased political knowledge or interest – and an intragroup path – defined by shared identities and agenda-setting – I will present research that proposes underlying processes of the aforementioned relations.

Following, I will extend the previous discourse and illustrate whether information that is gathered online has also an indirect effect on collective actions by evoking interactions between Internet users. Empirical evidence suggests four processes that are likely mediating the relation between information, discussion, and action: More frequent contact to weak ties and exposure to concrete calls for action as well as the formation and politicization of group identities.

Using the Internet to access information

Analyses of a representative sample of German Internet users over a period of seven years indicated that the most common type of Internet use is targeted information retrieval (i.e., between 61.4 and 64.5 per cent of the overall Internet use; Emmer, Vowe, & Wolling, 2011). Across the 28 member states of the European Union, 35 per cent of respondents of the European ICT survey used in 2011 the Internet to obtain information from public authorities; 40 per cent went online to read or download newspapers (Eurostat, 2014). Confirming this pattern, a study by the Pew Internet & American Life Project highlighted that between 2000 and 2008 the percentage of adults who acquired information about the US presidential campaign on the Internet grew from 16 to 40 per cent. Younger voters were inclined to learn about candidates and their political agendas on social network sites (Smith & Rainie, 2008).

The Internet grants unprecedented access to a variety of insights and news, from a range of sources that are not restricted by page limits or broadcasting times. National and international newspapers or television channels post videos, podcasts, and stories that often include material exclusively available in a digital format. Journalists share real-time updates of events, using (micro) blogging or content sharing platforms.

DOI: 10.1057/9781137440006.0006

Many alternative media outlets operate only on the Internet. Indy media – the Independent Media Center – for instance, represents a global network of journalists and citizens who use an open online publishing system to distribute content.

Finally, instead of relying on others to spread their message – possibly misinterpreting the mission or focusing on "sensational and uncivil protests" (Kim & Yoo, 2014, p. 145) – cause-related, advocacy, and social movement organizations can make use of Internet-enabled technologies to disseminate information about their activities, achievements, and agendas (Theocharis et al., 2013). In addition to websites and email (lists), social media platforms are important information brokers (Baumgartner & Morris, 2010); the latter offer grass-root organizations easy and free-of-charge possibilities to create a digital representation. Through Facebook pages, Twitter accounts, or YouTube channels, groups can address a large audience rapidly, multiple times a day. Compared to sending newsletters by post or contacting supporters by phone, the reach of information is enhanced and transmission costs are reduced.

Empowerment, knowledge, and interest

It has been postulated that as information spreads, so do contention and collective actions (Boulianne, 2009; Gordon, Baldwin-Philippi, & Balestra, 2013). Vasi and Suh (2013) showed in a study of the Occupy movement in the United States that gathering information – operationalized through the number of Google searches about the Occupy movement in a specific region – predicted whether or not a Facebook and Twitter account for a local Occupy group was registered. The latter increased the likelihood of protests on the ground. The relation between information and engagement can be studied from four angles, assessing the influence of a) political news, b) information about the agenda of a specific cause, c) practical information about collective actions, and d) live updates from (offline) activities.

For example, many insights about the uprisings in the Arab world were contributed by citizens who recorded the protests, attacks, arrests, or successes and posted the material immediately online. Lotan and colleagues (Lotan, Graeff, Ananny, Gaffney, & Pearce, 2011) identified the sources of tweets that were sent in January 2011 during the demonstrations in

Tunisia and Egypt and showed that bloggers, journalists, and self-defined activists were key to introducing and transferring live updates about the events. Notably, these individual voices were much louder than organizational posts. Although journalists and activists published most information on Twitter, bloggers and activists were more likely to circulate content via re-tweets. During the Gezi Park protests in Turkey, the majority of tweets, re-tweets, and replies referred to reports from the ground – political speeches or events in Gezi Park sparked the online activities (Varol, Ferrara, Ogan, Menczer, & Flammini, 2014).

To date, it is not yet supported that real-time information about collective actions encourages citizens who view the material to get engaged. It could, however, be speculated that photos, videos, or blog posts that cover ongoing events are empowering. Imagine, for instance, watching the live coverage of a sit-in where demonstrators are attacked by the police. For those who sympathize with the protesters' cause, witnessing the event as it evolves can have several consequences. First, it becomes clear how many people are actually engaged, emphasizing existing opinion and action support (Alberici & Milesi, 2013). It has been argued that individuals "decide not in parallel but sequentially [whether they join collective actions] (...) to see how many others are contributing" (González-Bailón et al., 2013). And previous research indicated that citizens were more likely to sign a petition if they knew that many others had already done so (i.e., reflecting a critical mass; Margetts, John, Escher, & Reissfelder, 2009). Especially those who did *not* strongly identify with a group were more willing to invest in a collective goal if the efforts of other members were communicated, demonstrating that it is worthwhile to work towards the collective interest (Fishbach, Henderson, & Koo, 2011). A randomized controlled trial with more than 61 million Facebook users further suggested that being informed about the collective actions of others – being shown whether Facebook friends had clicked the "I voted" button before the US congressional elections in 2010 – increased slightly (but significantly) users' likelihood to vote (i.e., an increase of .39 per cent; Bond et al., 2012).

To return to the previous example – viewing the live coverage of a sit-in where demonstrators are attacked by the police – real-time information about collective actions can also be empowering, because it highlights the rationale for participation. Collective actions are often set in an inter-group context where one group is – symbolically or literally – confronted by another. Conflicts may arise and call the attention of society at large

DOI: 10.1057/9781137440006.0006

to the issues that cause-related, advocacy, or social movement organizations are fighting for. The struggles provide additional legitimization for protests, boycotts, or campaigns and provide a platform to mobilize new supporters. More precisely, previous research suggested that individuals are likely to take collective actions if they arrive at the conclusion that a group is in an undeserved and unjust position (Martin, Brickman, & Murray, 1984). The latter may be experienced on behalf of a group that one affiliates with – fraternal or group-based injustice (Van Zomeren & Iyer, 2009) – or in solidarity of some other, disadvantaged group.

As citizens develop the interest to seek a solution to a collective concern, the Internet offers easy access to information about the practicalities and logistics of concrete actions. Verba, Schlozman, and Brady (1995) noted that less costly actions, which are easier, cheaper, or which require less cognitive and organizational resources, are more likely to be performed. In that sense, the Internet certainly reduces the costs and thereby the barriers of participation; important details of (offline or online) collective actions – where do actions take place, how to get there, what to bring – can be gathered within a split of a second, at any time, and from anywhere. In a study of the Step It Up national day of climate action in five locations across the United States, Fisher and Boekkooi (2010) reported that the Internet was for more than one third of the respondents the most important tool to learn about the activities. Especially citizens who were not formally affiliated with an environmental organization and who had no physical representation of the latter in their community relied on the Internet to arrange their participation.

Moreover, research endorsed that acquiring political news on the Internet promotes donations, volunteering, or rallying (Bimber, 2003; Boulianne, 2009; Gil de Zúñiga, Jung, & Valenzuela, 2012; Shah, Kwak, & Holbert, 2001; Valenzuela, Arriagada, & Sherman, 2012; Xenos & Moy, 2007). Boulianne (2009) demonstrated in a meta-analysis that if the measure of Internet use included online news access, its mean effect on political engagement yielded .13 ($p < .001$). Data from the American National Election Studies in 2004 revealed that learning about political campaigns online enhanced civic participation, for instance, working for an organization and taking part in a protest or in a march (Xenos & Moy, 2007). And using Facebook to watch, read, or listen to news was positively related to protests behaviour of young Chileans (Valenzuela et al., 2012).

DOI: 10.1057/9781137440006.0006

Exploring the underlying processes of these results, it has been postulated that gathering political news enhances individuals' awareness of relevant issues as well as learning (Eveland, Shah, & Kwak, 2003). The impact of information – accessed via newspapers and television or during interpersonal discussions – on political knowledge was demonstrated in a panel study (Eveland, Hayes, Shah, & Kwak, 2005). In a digital context, however, only selective knowledge – about the presidential primary candidate – was increased as a result of retrieving news on the Internet (Baumgartner & Morris, 2010). Importantly, the effect of knowledge on participation in collective actions has not been established.

More compelling evidence has been put forward for the facilitating role of political interest (Boulianne, 2009). Political news could mobilize those who are already interested in politics or encourage (as well) participation of previously uninvolved citizens. Boulianne (2011) showed in a panel study that access to online news amplified political interest and thereby political talk; political interest in turn did not impact the likelihood of gathering news on the Internet. The author explains that reading or listening to news online requires users to pay close attention and to process information deeply, which should strengthen interest in the subject matter.

Reading comments about political news enhanced further the likelihood to vote. Political interest moderated this influence as well as the impact of using Twitter for political purposes on voter turnout. The mobilizing effects were stronger for politically less interested respondents, suggesting that the latter benefited more from Internet use (Kruikemeier, van Noort, Vliegenthart, & de Vreese, 2013). Finally, Bimber and colleagues (2014) concluded – based on data from the British Election Studies – that the role of the Internet as a news source for voting increased between 2005 and 2010; it was in particular enhanced for those with low political interest (Bimber, Cunill, Copeland, & Gibson, 2014). Thus, it appears as if the "participation gap" (Bimber et al., 2014, p. 14) was narrowed, and citizens who were previously not interested in political matters were encouraged to take action.

The aforementioned discourse takes for granted that users search and encounter on the Internet information that is consistent with their sentiments and ideas. Individuals are inclined to endorse existing beliefs in order to avoid cognitive dissonance (Festinger, 1957); they also prefer interaction partners who are similar to themselves (Lazarsfeld & Merton, 1954) as these are expected to provide personal rewards and

DOI: 10.1057/9781137440006.0006

self-confirmation (Byrne & Clore, 1970; Condon & Crano, 1988). In many regards, the Internet facilitates the selection of information. Cass Sunstein stated that individuals are hearing "more and louder versions of their own pre-existing commitments" online (Sunstein, 2002, p. 185). In addition to visiting websites or social media accounts of sources that align with their point of view, algorithms customize, for instance, the results of search engines to inform users about things they "like". Nevertheless, the Internet is far less homogenous or balkanized as it is often claimed, and citizens are frequently exposed to opinions and news that might contest their perspectives. A study by the data science team of Facebook (Bakshy, 2012) emphasized that users received the majority of information on the social network site from so-called weak ties – individuals with whom they have less frequent contact and who are less similar to them (Granovetter, 1973). Weak ties introduce diverse and often counter-attitudinal information that could in fact undermine the mobilizing effect of information: Knobloch-Westerwick and Johnson (2014) reported that being exposed to novel but attitude-inconsistent information online reduced the willingness to take collective actions.

Identity formation and agenda setting

In addition to the previous intrapersonal argument, the impact of digital information on (offline) collective actions can also be addressed from a group-level perspective. Sharing information about their activities or achievements enables cause-related, advocacy, and social movement organizations to connect (potential) supporters to their mission (Lovejoy & Saxton, 2012). Engagement on behalf of a group requires understanding of what the group stands for, knowledge of the group's past, its goals, the relations to other groups, typical characteristics of group members as well as insights to rules and sanctioning mechanisms (Postmes, Haslam, & Swaab, 2005). As individuals identify with a group, these norms and self stereotypes govern their sentiments, decisions, and behaviour – in line with the group's purpose and aims (Turner et al., 1987).

Klein and colleagues (Klein, Spears, & Reicher, 2007) noted that "effective activists and leaders need to be skilled 'entrepreneurs of identity'" (p. 8) who shape the self-definition of those who ought to be mobilized. Very often this is done through rhetorical elements, rituals, and ceremonies, or negotiated in interactions. Likewise groups can construct

DOI: 10.1057/9781137440006.0006

identities and shape individuals' sense of membership through their web presence. Kavada (2012), drawing on Taylor and Every (2000), refers in this context to the Internet as a surface that represents the organization, its goals, stakeholders, or activities. In other words, by strategically curating the group's presentation on the Internet, a large number of individuals can be united around a shared norm that "enjoin(s) group members to act together in a way that is socially potent" (identity mobilization; Klein et al., 2007, p. 8). This argument resonates with the agenda setting approach to mass media that suggests that "there is a strong correlation between the emphasis that mass media place on certain issues (...) and the importance attributed to these issues" (Scheufele & Tewksbury, 2007, p. 11). Information that is more accessible ought to be processed more deeply and should ultimately steer behaviour (choices), including collective action tendencies.

In practice cause-related, advocacy, and social movement organizations often rely on storytelling to illustrate their work and achievements. Emotional and personal stories about stakeholders, the founders, or supporters of a grass-root organization convey vividly its core qualities. On the Internet, pictures, audio and video content can be added to complement text-heavy documentations. Beyond simply informing users, the stories allow citizens to relate to the cause and indicate concrete measures to turn this sense of involvement into action. charity:water show that this can be achieved in even less than one minute. The NGO demonstrates its campaigns on its website in a short video, highlighting the status-quo – for example, the drought in the Sahel zone in Africa – and challenge that ought to be addressed – providing 100,000 people with access to clean water. Showing the struggles of the women in the Sahel zone, who spend every day hours trying to find water for their families, touches the viewers and pronounces the relevance of the issue. To follow up on the need to act, citizens can immediately start a fundraising campaign or sponsor a project by clicking icons that are placed just below the video.

From information to (inter)actions

Information may be a currency of power, but it "is most valuable when it can be put to use in voicing and discussing opinions" (Gordon et al., 2013, p. 3). Indeed, a quintessential element of the Internet – ever since it gained popularity – are systems that enable computer-mediated

DOI: 10.1057/9781137440006.0006

communication, systems that connect users in synchronous or asynchronous interactions. From the first email that Ray Tomlinson sent to himself in 1971 to today's platforms and Internet services, the functions and features certainly advanced. Users no longer need to be online at the same time to receive an email. And messages are addressed – including sophisticated (or slightly less sophisticated) non-verbal symbols such as emoticons – to one or multiple users, all within a split second. The core idea, however, remained the same: CMC allows individuals to share information and encourages the exchange of opinions without limits of time or space.

As noted earlier, when scholars examine the patterns and consequences of Internet use, they often distinguish specific types as suggested by the uses and gratification approach (Katz et al., 1974). For instance, in a study of youths' Facebook use and protest behaviour, Valenzuela and colleagues (2012) assessed to what extent respondents employed the social network site for retrieving news, expressing opinions, and organizing their social life. These different digital practices are not independent but overlap, are performed simultaneously, or determine one another.[4] The communication mediation model (Sotirovic & McLeod, 2001) adopts this notion and argues, more precisely, that gathering information online prompts offline collective actions by encouraging users to reflect on the issues they read about, motivating interactions in chat rooms, forums, or on social network sites. Acquiring information may raise controversies that stimulate dialogue (Shah, Cho, Eveland, & Kwak, 2005), it enables users to participate in discussions more persuasively, and can promote thorough reasoning that underlies the decision to take collective actions (Nah, Veenstra, & Shah., 2006). Nah and colleagues (2006) examined the impact of political news and discussion on activism against the war in Iraq. Reading newspapers and searching for information about the situation in Iraq on the Internet drove online and face-to-face political discussions which both predicted displaying a banner, donating to an activist organization, and joining a protest or rally. But how can this complex relation be explained?

Weak ties

Engaging (with) fellow users or representatives of a cause-related, advocacy, or social movement organization in digital dialogue brings users

DOI: 10.1057/9781137440006.0006

together in loose communities that have the potential to stage collective actions. Gil de Zúñiga and Valenzuela (2011) highlighted that Internet use enhanced volunteering for a non-political group or fundraising for a charity by increasing the likelihood to interact with weak ties; the latter had a larger impact on civic engagement than strong ties. As a reminder, weak ties refer to relationships that are defined by low emotional intensity, intimacy, or reciprocity, and they are a source of diverse insights, connecting clusters of strong ties – such as family members – that hold mostly redundant information (Granovetter, 1973). Face-to-face encounters foster as well weak tie connections (see Gil de Zúñiga & Valenzuela, 2011). But the Internet – and in particular social network sites such as Facebook – enables individuals to establish and manage weak tie relations much more efficiently, enhancing also the scope and speed with which the information that is available within the network can be accessed.

As users are part of ever-growing digital networks, they are more likely to meet others who are already active for a cause and who can point out concrete calls for action (Eveland & Hively, 2009). Klandermans (1997) suggested that in order to join collective actions, individuals first need to identify with an initiative or group. Before developing the motivation to act and overcoming barriers of engagement, citizens also have to be targeted by mobilizing efforts. In fact, being explicitly asked to attend action might be one of the strongest predictors for participation (Verba et al., 1995).

Forming, strengthening, and politicizing group identities

Similar to the intrapersonal and intragroup paths that I proposed for the relation between information and collective actions, the mobilizing influence of online discussions can be approached from a group perspective. In particular interactions among like-minded users can elicit a bottom-up process of group formation or identity construction (Postmes, Haslam, et al., 2005; Postmes, Spears, et al., 2005). Based on the arguments or non-verbal and para-verbal elements of communication that are exchanged in interactions, users can infer what others value and strive for. By negotiating personal opinions, individuals

DOI: 10.1057/9781137440006.0006

recognize similarities and build on these to arrive at shared impressions that shape the group's norms and the understanding of what it means to belong to this group. In addition, the constituents of a group's identity may be discussed explicitly; as these interactions continue, group identities remain to be sharpened. Kavada (2012) noted that "web 2.0 platforms problematize the notion of the 'organization' as an already formed (...) actor" (p. 5); user-generated content must be constantly integrated in the architecture of the group. Group goals emerge and prescribe concrete practices or broader frames within which supporters may act.

Once group identities are established, individuals' sense of belonging may be further strengthened through deliberations on the Internet, especially if group members remain anonymous. The social identity model of deindividuation effects (SIDE) proposes that immersion in a crowd or anonymity within a group increases social regulation (Spears & Lea, 1994; Spears, Postmes, Lea, & Wolbert, 2002). More precisely, drawing on self-categorization and social identity theory (Tajfel & Turner, 1979; Turner et al., 1987), the so-called cognitive effect of SIDE describes how anonymity impacts the "accessibility of contextually relevant identities" (Spears et al., 2002, p. 95). Given that a particular group membership is salient – being explicitly stated or contextually derived – the limited availability of interpersonal cues and obscured individual differences of interaction partners enhances the salience of the respective social identity. Previous research supported this postulation, indicating that group discussions that were set in an anonymous context increased the social influence (Postmes, Spears, Sakhel, & De Groot, 2001) and perceived entitativity of a group (Sassenberg & Postmes, 2002) as well as group identification (Lea, Spears, & De Groot, 2001) and attraction (Spears et al., 2002); it further fostered attitude polarization in line with group norms (Spears, Lea, & Lee, 1990).

Last but not least, studies of protest movements in Italy pointed out that online interactions among like-minded users who identified with a cause affected the likelihood to join demonstrations by moderating the impact of group members' sense of injustice, identification, perceived group efficacy, moral outrage, and anger (Alberici & Milesi, 2013). Voicing anger about the unjust situation of their group on the Internet reduced the effect of this group-based emotion on offline collective actions, while the influence of moral outrage and perceived group efficacy was

DOI: 10.1057/9781137440006.0006

enhanced. Importantly, the discussions stimulated the politicization of collective identities (Simon & Klandermans, 2001).

Politicized forms of identity have a strong normative content and are related to an activist identity (Van Zomeren, Postmes, & Spears, 2012); they are "a form of collective identity that underlies group members' explicit motivations to [intentionally] engage in (...) a power struggle" with other groups (Simon & Klandermans, 2001, p. 323). Simon and Klandermans (2001) postulated that in order to develop politicized collective identities, group members need to experience a sense of shared grievance, that is, agree that their group is treated unfairly or that the group's principles are violated. Second, the reason for this grievance must be blamed on a specific outgroup. In order to overcome the struggle, compensations are demanded from the outgroup. If the latter does not give in to the requests, the issue may be taken to a more comprehensive level by asking authorities or society as a whole to take sides. Once third parties get engaged in the power struggle – a triangulation – collective identities become politicized. Simon and Klandermans (2001) emphasize the agency function of politicized collective identities; "having forced society or its representatives to take sides confers recognition as a social agent on group members" (p. 328) which should encourage further collective actions. Indeed, identification with politicized groups predicted participation in collective actions stronger than identification with broader social categories (i.e., identification with the Gay movement as compared to identification with gay men) (Stürmer & Simon, 2004; Stürmer, Simon, Loewy, & Jörger, 2003).

How can online interactions enhance the politicization of identities and thereby increase the likelihood of collective actions? First, deliberations on the Internet enable a large number of individuals to arrive more quickly at the conclusion that – based on their group membership – they are treated unjustly. A digital context also facilitates the negotiation on whether an outgroup is to be blamed for the group's struggle, involving more supporters from different locations and time zones than feasible in face-to-face discussions. Finally, the Internet facilitates the politicization of identities, because third parties can be more easily brought on board. Group discussions are often public and permanently accessible on the Internet. Politicians, other citizens, and civil society are hence more likely to be exposed to a group's mission. Especially social network,

DOI: 10.1057/9781137440006.0006

(micro) blogging, and content sharing platforms encourage the dissemination of information within users' personal networks; ultimately groups can reach out and demand support from large segments of society at low costs.

Take home message

The Internet incites offline collective actions by providing quick and easy access to information – to political news, real-time updates from collective actions, practical information as well as information about the goals and norms of organizations that initiate collective actions. Intrapersonal as well intragroup processes could drive this mobilizing effect. On the one hand, the costs of participation are reduced and political interest is enhanced. On the other hand, information about cause-related, advocacy, and social movement organizations explicitly defines the group's identity and makes it easier for new supporters to be quickly integrated in the campaign. Concluding, the most common type of Internet use – retrieving information or lurking – is likely shaping the scale of collective actions.

Information that is gathered online prompts dialogues with fellow users through email, in chat rooms, forums, or on social network sites. These online discussions foster connections with weak ties and encourage exposure to direct calls for action. Moreover, joining interactions on the Internet shapes processes of group formation that incite offline collective actions. Group norms can emerge and prescribe collective action tactics; identification with a group may be strengthened if deliberations take place in an anonymous context, and finally, group identities are more likely to politicize.

Notes

1   See, for instance, Van Zomeren, Postmes, and Spears, 2008, for a meta-analysis of predictors of collective actions.
2   The use of traditional media – newspaper, television, or radio – is strongly defined by content consumption; the participatory Internet, however, also encourages co-production and participation, extending the possibly types of media use (Macafee & De Simone, 2012).

DOI: 10.1057/9781137440006.0006

3 Gathering information from newspapers and joining controversial face-to-face discussions promoted as well participation; watching television for entertainment purposes also foreclosed engagement (Sotirovic & McLeod, 2001).

4 Valenzuela and colleagues (2012) report significant correlations between the three practices.

3

The Internet as a Platform for Online Collective Actions

Abstract: *The Internet shapes individuals' repertoires of contention by offering a platform for collective actions such as online petitions or donations. Chapter 3 introduces digital practices that aim to advance a solution to collective struggles, focusing on tactics that are available to all Internet users and that pose low risks. Especially users who lack the resources to join offline actions and supporters who prefer to follow individual action frames may be encouraged to get engaged on the Internet. In the second part of the chapter, I discuss the drawbacks of convenient online collective actions. More precisely, I assess the slacktivism hypothesis which proposes that low-threshold online collective actions foreclose enduring participation. Findings from three experiments endorse this postulation and highlight that quick and easy Internet based collective actions are considered as equally valid and potent as offline engagement.*

Schumann, Sandy. *How the Internet Shapes Collective Actions*. Basingstoke: Palgrave Macmillan, 2015.
DOI: 10.1057/9781137440006.0007.

The Internet has been hailed as a liberation technology that empowers and strengthens civil society (Diamond, 2010). Most commonly, this claim refers to the facilitating function of the Internet, that is, the notion that Internet use fosters offline collective actions. Technological advancements and accompanying shifts in the Internet use culture, however, give an impetus to extend this perspective and to consider the Internet as a platform for collective actions. In the following chapter, I will discuss practices of online collective actions, focusing on examples that are available to everyone with Internet access. To date, digital tactics of contention are not yet theoretically conceptualized, and it is often unclear whether users actually view particular acts – for instance, "liking" a Facebook post of an advocacy group – as a means to work towards a collective purpose. I present findings from a questionnaire study that highlight four types of Internet-based collective actions; these include easy click-based actions as well as digital equivalents of traditional forms of collective actions such as petitions.

Moreover, I will address the lively debate around the phenomenon of slacktivism and the postulation that convenient collective actions on the Internet are nothing more than slacker or arm-chair activism, making users feel good about themselves and foreclosing enduring participation in collective actions (Gladwell, 2010; Morozov, 2009). I will introduce results from three experiments that support this substitute hypothesis, but that nuance as well the slacktivism proposition. More precisely, I will point out that the satisfaction of group-focused motivations – the need to contribute to the group's success – mediates the demobilizing impact of clicks and "likes".

Patterns of Internet-based collective actions

"A fresh wave of technological optimism has more recently accompanied the advent of social media platforms such as Twitter, Facebook, YouTube, Wikies and the blogosphere" (Loader & Mercea, 2011, p. 758), also, because the Internet provides a vibrant infrastructure for digital repertoires of contention. This diffusion of protest-related innovations (Earl, 2010) seems to be a natural shift in a society where the Internet is becoming increasingly interwoven in everyday life (Krotoski, 2013). Especially social media platforms "have been found to be the most common gateway into digital activism" (Harlow & Guo, 2014, p. 1).

DOI: 10.1057/9781137440006.0007

Some tactics, for instance, hacktivism – changing the source code of a website or introducing malicious software – are specific to the virtual context (Van Laer & Van Aelst, 2010). Other practices are extensions of offline collective actions. Consider platforms such as Change.org that enable citizens and civil society to easily set up and circulate online petitions. Online donations can be collected through websites such as VirginMoneyGiving – systems that offer tools to promote campaigns and transfer funds. Culture jamming is another way to advance a collective purpose; corporate logos or slogans are altered in an artistic fashion, a process which is much easier when using digital tools (Van Laer & Van Aelst, 2010). And rather than wearing a button or putting up a banner, individuals can signal their endorsement for a cause or organization through "liking", "favourites", and by "joining" Facebook pages.

The majority of the aforementioned examples require little time and pose low risks to users. Van Laer and Van Aelst (2010) therefore refer to such Internet-based collective actions as low-threshold actions. The latter are distinguished from high-threshold actions – such as hacktivism – that are risky and for which a high level of involvement or particular skills are necessary. In the following, I will focus only on low-threshold online collective actions that are widely available to all Internet users.[1] Little is known about the conceptualization of these Internet-based collective actions. Some dismiss "liking" a post on Facebook or signing an online petition as slacker-activism – a phenomenon that I will elaborate on in more detail in the second part of the chapter. Supporters of cause-related, advocacy, and social movement organizations, however, might consider said actions as substantial engagement to advance a collective purpose, allowing also those to take action who do not have the resources – time, money, or organizational skills – to participate offline (Vissers, Hooghe, Stolle, & Mahéo, 2011).

In order to develop a better understanding of the nature and perception of low-threshold online collective actions, I invited supporters of the environmental advocacy group Greenpeace to report their Internet use patterns in an online questionnaire. Six hundred and twenty respondents (65.6 per cent female; $M = 30.05$ ($SD = 11.30$) years old (range: 14 – 78 years)) indicated how frequently they had used in the past different features of the web presence of Greenpeace as well as their personal accounts on social media platforms. The organization's websites, the social media platforms Facebook, Twitter, and YouTube, Greenpeace email lists, and personal blogs and email accounts were included in the analyses. Examples of the

DOI: 10.1057/9781137440006.0007

digital practices that were assessed are: Gathering information from the Greenpeace website, Signing a petition on Greenpeace website, "Liking" a post by Greenpeace on their Facebook page, or Indicating a tweet by Greenpeace as a "favorite".

Online behaviour that has been referred to as Internet-based collective actions – making donations, signing petitions, expressing support through "likes" and equivalent symbolic acts or written statements as well as practices of sharing information with one's personal network – were included in a principal component analysis with Varimax rotation and Kaiser normalization.[2] The findings highlight four independent factors (Table 3.1). Following calls for actions to sign online petitions via Facebook or Greenpeace email list emerged as one factor (eigenvalue: 1.65), as did making an online donation on the website and through Greenpeace Facebook page (eigenvalue: 1.16). The remaining two factors (factor 1 with an eigenvalue of 8.63, factor 2 with an eigenvalue of 2.07) hold mixed activities such as expressing support through a photo or banner, signing petitions on Greenpeace website, and sharing information about Greenpeace with one's personal network on Facebook – the latter two practices loaded on the same factor.

Factor four may be considered as an Internet-based collective action that is instrumental and that contributes tangible means – money – to the organization (Freelon, 2014). Factor three represents online petitions, expressive collective actions that signal respondents' support for Greenpeace (Melucci, 1996). These symbolic tactics also define factors one and two, even though the patterns are less systematic. Nevertheless, these results suggest that digital equivalents of group-brokered collective actions are considered as equivalent to more self-organized (connective) actions that are facilitated by social network sites – sharing information about a cause with one's personal network. Both practices address a collective struggle and promote Greenpeace solution to protect and conserve the environment. Thus, the distinction between organization-brokered and crowd-enabled collective actions might be in practice less pronounced than theoretically proposed. Citizens seem to combine different strategies in their repertoires of contention and draw on specific tactics depending on their resources, agreement with a particular campaign, or the organizational interpretation of an issue.

Generally speaking, the Internet diversifies the opportunities of involvement for experienced supporters and breaks down barriers of

DOI: 10.1057/9781137440006.0007

TABLE 3.1 *Rotated Component Matrix*

Digital Practice	Factor			
	1	2	3	4
Website: Sign a petition	.701	.090	.557	-.017
Facebook profile/newsfeed: Share Greenpeace posts with your network	.649	.409	.195	.241
Facebook profile/newsfeed: Express your support for Greenpeace in your profile or cover photo	.718	.523	-.069	.125
Facebook profile/newsfeed: Commit to events organized by Greenpeace	.741	.213	.271	.260
Facebook page: "Like" Greenpeace posts	.724	.450	.247	-.074
Twitter: Express your support for Greenpeace in your banner and profile photo	.703	.485	-.142	.258
Twitter: Share information about Greenpeace and its activities with your followers	.786	.357	.256	-.231
Personal email: Express your support for Greenpeace to your friends and family	.744	.310	.319	.020
YouTube: "Like" Greenpeace videos	.364	.718	.240	.020
YouTube: Share Greenpeace videos on other social media platforms	.376	.791	.147	.030
Twitter: "Favorite" Greenpeace tweets	.364	.590	.485	.037
Personal YouTube Channel: Express support for Greenpeace and its activities in your videos	.186	.715	-.221	.441
Personal Blog: Express support for Greenpeace and its activities in your posts	.292	.775	.112	-.385
Facebook page: Follow calls to sign petitions	.149	.587	.742	.012
Email list: Follow calls of action	.195	-.048	.891	.048
Website: Make a donation	-.031	.065	.167	.888
Facebook page: Make donations	.558	-.117	-.177	.676

Note: Bold numbers indicate on which factor the respective digital practice load.

participation for previously unengaged citizens (Tufekci, 2012), enhancing the overall scale of collective actions. And it may not stop there. In recent years, the cross-medium spillover of the low-threshold online collective actions that I assessed in the aforementioned study has been discussed. More precisely, it has been proposed that the low-cost and low-risk digital practices provide a stepping stone, a rung on a ladder of engagement that incites subsequent (offline) engagement.

Indeed, using social media to promote a social or political cause predicted volunteering, making donations (Waggener Edstrom Worldwide

Inc. & Georgetown University, 2013), joining demonstrations (Macaffe, 2012), and voting (Vitak et al., 2011). More than 24 per cent of citizens who were engaged in grass-root civic, social, and religious groups (*N* = 2303) indicated that they had volunteered more frequently and had donated more money due to the Internet; 41 per cent noted that Internet use had improved their ability to organize events for the group (Rainie et al., 2011). Vissers and Stolle (2012) further showed that expressing political opinions on Facebook fostered donations and contacting politicians offline; "liking" or "joining" Facebook groups of political parties prompted protesting. Finally, after signing an online petition for a charity, participants pledged more money to charities that addressed a similar cause as the petition and were more willing to sign another petition or to write letters to politicians (Lee & Hsieh, 2013; see also Guéguen & Jacob, 2002).

The challenge or opportunity of slacktivism

As mentioned earlier, the examples of online collective actions that I addressed thus far have in common that they are available to everyone with Internet access, that they are easy and often relatively quick to perform, and that they pose few risks. Despite the promising mobilizing potential of these low-threshold online collective actions, questions have been raised as to whether the latter may not hold hidden costs and crowd out enduring engagement (Karpf, 2010). In a more extreme tone, Evgeny Morozov (2009) noted that low-threshold online actions are "the ideal type of activism for a lazy generation". The "*many clicks*" (p. 2) are viewed as banal forms of participation (Lim, 2013) and referred to as slacktivism, a negative connoted term that is constructed of the words slacker and activism (Leonard, 2009). Citizens who engage in low-threshold online collective actions are criticized for not wanting "to get their hands dirty" (Christensen, 2011, para. 28) and for lacking the passion and dedication of supporters who are active offline (Harlow & Guo, 2014).

Moreover, low-threshold online collective actions are proposed to make users instantly feel good about themselves, to elevate their self-esteem, and to satisfy the need to take action (Morozov, 2009) – as a consequence, future collective actions could be foreclosed (Lee & Hsieh, 2013). Initial support for this substitute effect of so-called slacktivist actions was put forward by Kristofferson and colleagues; the authors demonstrated that participants thought that they had made a positive impression on an audience by taking public low-threshold collective actions, which decreased the likelihood of further engagement for the same cause (Kristofferson, White, & Peloza, 2014).

To complement this evidence I conducted three experiments[3] and examined whether, indeed, taking low-threshold online collective actions reduces the willingness to join subsequent (offline) collective actions. Students at a Belgian university were invited to take part in a study that assessed their perception of the need to protect the environment. Participants reported first their pro-environmental attitudes. They then were informed that their opinions were similar to these of members of an environmental group; the group was given a specific name and referred to as "your" group. The context of the study thus suggested a group-brokered collective action that was defined by the agenda and goals of a formal group – in this case, the goal to preserve biodiversity and establish a natural reserve.

All participants were asked to visit the website of their group to learn more about its activities and achievements. Half of the students only read the information presented on the website and were then immediately directed to a second questionnaire. The other half of students was asked to take – in addition to reading the material on the website – a low-threshold online collective action. More precisely, participants were instructed to express support for their group in a comment that would be posted on the website, visible to other members. The length of the comment was not restricted. Upon posting the comment, the participants in the experimental condition also completed the second questionnaire. The latter assessed participants' willingness to join a panel discussion and demonstration as well as to what degree participants felt as if they contributed to their group's success, felt good about themselves, and thought that they were accepted by fellow group members. Last but not least, participants had the opportunity to sign a (paper) petition.

The results indicated that participants who stated their support for the environmental group on the Internet were *less* willing to join subsequent offline collective actions and were *less* likely to sign the petition on behalf of their group. This demobilizing effect was mediated by a reduced sense of responsibility; participants who took the low-threshold online collective action believed more strongly that they contributed to their group's welfare and goal attainment, which is why they were less willing to remain to be engaged. The findings could be considered as support

DOI: 10.1057/9781137440006.0007

of the slacktivism critique, support of the idea that taking quick and easy collective actions online forecloses enduring participation, as users believe they have done enough to advance a collective goal. The results, however, also highlight that participants took their group – its goals, progress, and viability – into account and did not refrain from acting offline due to hedonistic motives.

Moreover, low-threshold online collective actions affect offline engagement, because both practices address the same needs. In turn, it can be concluded that low-cost and low-risk online collective actions are viewed as legitimate tactics (Gil de Zúñiga, Veenstra, Vraga, & Shah, 2010), as part of individuals' repertoire of contention. The medium of action – the Internet – should not be confounded with the level of commitment of those who act. In conclusion, online and offline behaviour should be understood as integrated and coordinated, not distinguished as set in the digital and the "real" world.

Take home message

The Internet diversifies individuals' repertoire of contention by providing a platform for Internet-based collective actions. The latter resemble digital extensions of offline tactics, such as petitions and donations, but include as well actions that are unique to the virtual context. Online collective actions often entail low costs and risks for users. Individuals who cannot invest the resources to take collective actions offline may be inclined to get involved for a cause on the Internet. Supporters who are already engaged can expand their actions repertoires through instrumental and expressive digital practices. Low-threshold online collective actions seem to address the same needs as demonstrations or signing paper petitions, for instance: and are viewed as an equally valid measure to ensure that a group achieves its goals. Therefore, however, quick and easy Internet-based collective actions may also foreclose enduring participation.

Notes

1 Although it is not covered here in more detail, hacktivism is an important facet of the spectrum of online collective actions and should not be dismissed

DOI: 10.1057/9781137440006.0007

as cybercrime. Interested readers should view the TED talk of Keren Elazari (2014) who described hackers as the immune system of the Internet, defending Internet security and freedom.

2 See Schumann and Klein (in press) for a detailed description of the study.

3 For a more detailed overview of the studies, see Schumann and Klein (in press).

DOI: 10.1057/9781137440006.0007

4

How Cause-related, Advocacy, and Social Movement Organizations Use the Internet to Promote Collective Actions

Abstract: *Cause-related, advocacy, and social movement organizations are increasingly establishing sophisticated web presences that include websites, email lists as well as social media accounts. In Chapter 4, I review the current digital practices of grass-root organizations; their Internet use patterns include information dissemination, community-building, and the promotion of organizational-brokered or crowd-enabled collective actions. Following, I discuss how these activities align with the expectations and aspirations of stakeholders who want to engage with a cause or initiative online. Especially information transfer is appreciated by supporters, but does not contribute to their sense of involvement. In conclusion, organizations are advised to diversify their digital campaigns to harness the mobilizing potential of the Internet more efficiently.*

Schumann, Sandy. *How the Internet Shapes Collective Actions.* Basingstoke: Palgrave Macmillan, 2015.
DOI: 10.1057/9781137440006.0008.

DOI: 10.1057/9781137440006.0008

Theoretical arguments as well as empirical evidence suggest that the Internet can shape the nature and scale of collective actions. To recap, the participatory Internet encourages self-organized and decentralized connective actions. In addition, gathering information and interacting with like-minded users online fosters participation in collective actions offline. Finally, especially social media platforms diversify individuals' repertoires of contention and provide a platform for Internet-based collective actions. In order to harness the full potential of the Internet, cause-related, advocacy, and social movement organizations that aim to mobilize citizens might be expected to consider these insights, that is, invest in a web presence that focuses on sharing information, that encourages interactions, and offers means to express individual action frames.

In this chapter, I will take a closer look at the digital practices of grass-root organizations and activists to showcase how the latter use social media platforms or Internet services to promote engagement. I will not repeat suggestions from handbooks or guidelines that prescribe appropriate strategies; rather, I will consider studies that evaluate current Internet use patterns. Moreover, I will report findings from a questionnaire study as well as my own research that examine how influential and involving supporters perceive different digital repertoires of contention.

Digital mobilizing practices

Analyzing the Twitter use of 100 US-American non-profit organizations, Lovejoy and Saxton (2012) suggested a suitable framework to discuss the digital mobilizing practices of cause-related, advocacy, and social movement organizations. The authors identified three principal types of use – information, community, and actions – that represent a ladder of engagement. Initially, users are informed about the goals and agenda of the organization. Second, citizens become part of and connected with a larger community of supporters to establish a sense of membership; finally, taking the third step, they can act on this notion of belonging and join collective actions. Guo and Saxton (2014) referred to this progressive approach also as a pyramid model that includes reaching out to people, keeping their flame alive, and helping them to realize their action tendencies.

In order to respond to supporters who do not know yet a group's mission and to acknowledge at the same time those who already identify

DOI: 10.1057/9781137440006.0008

with the group's purpose, the three stages of engagement are ideally addressed simultaneously. Nevertheless, especially mobilizing efforts for concrete actions, such as promoting attendance at an event or calling for volunteers and lobbying, are rare (Lovejoy & Saxton, 2012); they represented only 11.6 per cent of the tweets of non-profit organizations that were assessed by Guo and Saxton (2014). Across different studies that included a variety of social media platforms and Internet services, the most common organizational digital practice was information dissemination. Representatives of 53 advocacy groups indicated in a study by Obar, Zube, and Lampe (2012) that Facebook and Twitter are used to educate the public about central issues or to inform stakeholders about important dates and events. Advocacy organizations consider in particular social media platforms as a means to strengthen outreach efforts at an unprecedented speed and at low costs. Moreover, with the help of social media platforms, organizations can operate outside their regular realm of influence; they can more easily join the public discourse and therefore are more likely to be visible to potential supporters. Consequently, organizational growth is enhanced. In line with this argument, Rainie and colleagues (2011) showed that 57 per cent of Internet users in their sample had been invited online to join a social, civic, professional, or religious group.

Lovejoy and Saxton (2012) further highlighted that more than half of the tweets sent by non-profit organizations were intended to share insights and news, and 47 of the 100 organizations that were included in the study were primarily sharing information. In Guo and Saxton's (2014) study even 70 per cent of the tweets were used to spread information. Transnational non-governmental organizations reported that blogs, wikis or video, and podcasts were an important tool to promote the image of the organization, to raise funds, and to provide information to journalists. The latter was more important than interactions with the public (Seo, Kim, & Yang, 2009). In fact, a content analysis of the Facebook postings of 275 non-profit organizations in the United States indicated that the organizations used the discussion wall of their Facebook group mainly to pass on information or to post links to external stories (Waters, Burnett, Lamm, & Lucas, 2008).

Also crowd-enabled actions rely on the Internet as a means to disseminate information. Kim and colleagues (2014) studied the online behaviour of self-proclaimed activists and citizens on the Facebook page of the Gangjeong movement in China. The activists used the Facebook

DOI: 10.1057/9781137440006.0008

page mainly to share firsthand observations from the protests; posts by citizens were aimed at mobilizing others through supportive and inspirational messages. Activists put up hyperlinks to alternative news sources; citizens used these to connect with activists or other social movement organizations and to transfer the message of the campaign to their personal social networks.

Overall, interactions between supporters and organizational representatives are much less common, but still an important element of the digital practices of cause-related, advocacy, and social movement organizations (Bortee & Seltzer, 2009; Lovejoy & Saxton, 2012). For instance, on Twitter, gratitude and recognition are expressed by re-tweeting, by answering to messages, or by encouraging users to respond to requests and questions. In Guo and Saxton's (2014) analysis, tweets that were targeted towards building a community or related to stakeholders made up 19.73 per cent of the posts. Through these interactions, groups hope to develop unifying and engaging feedback loops (Obar et al., 2012), gaining insights about supporters' opinions and personal interpretations of the organizations' activities. At the same time, as has been pointed out in more detail in Chapter 2, dialogue between organizations and supporters enable groups to establish connections, build communities, and define identities.

There are two possible reasons why interactions with stakeholders are less frequent than top-down information transfer. First, the aforementioned analyses refer to the Internet use patterns of formal groups that aim to mobilize citizens for organization-brokered actions. As noted, in this context, supporters are less flexible to negotiate personalized paths of engagement (Bennett & Segerberg, 2012, 2013). Rather, the group is setting an agenda – this is achieved by disseminating information and not through deliberation between users. An emphasis on sharing information online might thus be a strategic decision in order to establish clear collective action frames.

Alternatively, organizations may not believe that meaningful bonds can be established online. Harlow and Guo (2014) reported that employees and volunteers of organizations that assist immigrants did not consider social media as a tool to relate in a sustainable way to their supporters and beneficiaries. The organizations used Facebook, Twitter, YouTube, websites, Skype, emails, blogs, or listservers to approach general public, other activist organizations, officials, power holders, or immigrants themselves (Harlow & Guo, 2014). All platforms and Internet services

DOI: 10.1057/9781137440006.0008

were, however, primarily viewed as means to raise awareness and not to incite actions. Overall, the interviewees were not convinced that digital dialogue alone could help grow the strong personal connections that are necessary to encourage sustainable engagement (see Gladwell, 2010).

The supporters' perspective

The aforementioned organizational practices are intended to inform, engage, and mobilize supporters. But does the online outreach of cause-related, advocacy, and social movement organizations actually meet citizens' expectations? In "Assessing the Dynamics of Cause Engagement", Waggener International and The Center for Social Impact Communication at Georgetown University (2011) showed that only 18 per cent of the respondents got initially involved for a cause on social media platforms – by "joining" the Facebook group of a cause, posting its logo, or writing about it; donating money, talking with others about the respective cause, and learning about the issues that the cause addresses were the most common forms of initial involvement. As social media platforms are expected to become increasingly popular amongst grass-root organizations and stakeholders, the authors conclude that it is certainly advised to further develop digital campaigns. In making reference to crowd-enabled collective actions, the report also suggests that it would be beneficial to offer opportunities for participation online and offline, allowing supporters to choose tactics that align with collective or personal action frames.

These findings highlight how likely it is that citizens use social media platforms as a means for engagement. The study provides, however, no insights into perceptions of digital practices. For instance, do users value the manifold information that grass-root organizations post online? And are different Internet-based collective actions – expressive and instrumental tactics – considered as equally influential for advancing a collective purpose? In order to respond to these questions, I conducted a questionnaire study in which I asked participants how influential they thought different online behaviour were for achieving a group's goal, and how involved they would feel if they took these actions on the Internet. Supporters of the environmental advocacy group Greenpeace answered both questions with reference to the following behaviours[1]: Signing online petitions, Donating money online, Verbally expressing support for Greenpeace online (e.g., on Facebook, Twitter, personal emails, or blogs), Sharing calls of action with friends and family via email or social media platforms, Creating videos to express support for Greenpeace, Getting information about Greenpeace and its activities, Giving feedback to Greenpeace on social media platforms (e.g., "Liking" Greenpeace posts on Facebook), and Interacting with other Greenpeace supporters.

The descriptive results of the analysis are presented in Table 4.1. Receiving information about Greenpeace activities was viewed as the most influential practice, even more so than signing petitions online ($t(572) = -3.36$, $p = .00$). Creating videos to express support for Greenpeace was rated as least influential. Knowing about the organization's latest developments and achievements, supporters might feel that they can make informed decisions and steer their group towards its goals. The relevance of information access resonates with the practices of cause-related, advocacy, and social movement groups that focus primarily on information dissemination.

At the same time, this "match" could hold hidden costs: As indicated in Chapter 3, if users consider their online behaviour as a meaningful contribution to a group's success, they are likely to refrain from subsequent engagement. With this in mind, the findings propose possible boundary conditions of this substitute effect. More precisely, when being asked which online behaviour would make them feel most involved with Greenpeace, respondents reported interactions with other supporters, sharing calls for action, and expressing support for Greenpeace online. That is, supporters seem to appreciate interactive features of the participatory Internet as tools to act upon their sense of belonging to the organization. By joining dialogues with fellow citizens and taking expressive online collective actions, individuals strengthen their affiliation with the group and establish an enduring need for involvement.

Cause-related, advocacy, and social movement organizations thus benefit from encouraging interactions between supporters, from allowing users to share material with their personal network, and from offering opportunities to express support on the Internet. These practices could prompt bonds with and between stakeholders, building a network of individuals or initiatives that constitutes a powerful source of influence. Organizations appear to be still critical about the community-building potential of the Internet. But it seems as if interested citizens are not having these doubts: They are inclined to take digital paths to become involved with an organization. Future research is necessary to endorse

DOI: 10.1057/9781137440006.0008

TABLE 4.1   *Perceived influence and involvement of digital practices*

Digital Practice	Perceived Influence		Perceived Involvement	
	M	SD	M	SD
Signing online petitions	4.44	1.34	4.04	1.43
Donating money online	4.43	1.32	3.91	1.56
Verbally expressing your support for Greenpeace online (e.g., on Facebook, Twitter, personal email)	4.25	1.36	4.20	1.37
Sharing calls of action with your friends and family via email or social media platforms	4.21	1.33	4.19	1.36
Creating videos to express support for Greenpeace	3.77	1.51	4.00	1.62
Getting information about Greenpeace and its activities	4.66	1.27	4.03	1.40
Giving feedback to Greenpeace on social media platforms (e.g., "Liking" Greenpeace posts on Facebook)	4.07	1.47	3.88	1.44
Interacting with other Greenpeace supporters	4.08	1.45	4.21	1.53

Note: Participants reported their opinions on a six-point scale (1 = *not at all influential/ involving*; 6 = *very influential/involving*).

the aforementioned results. Nevertheless, it is evident that in order to harness the mobilizing power of the Internet all possible rungs of the ladder of engagement – informing about goals, building a community, and proposing concrete actions – must be addressed.

Take home message

Cause-related, advocacy, and social movement organizations are increasingly implementing sophisticated web presences and establish social media accounts. Analyses of these digital practices, however, highlight that the organizations are not yet taking full advantage of the interactive features that the platforms or Internet services offer. Information dissemination remains, to date, the most popular type of Internet use. This pattern resonates with citizens' expectations – they view retrieving information about a group's activities as influential, as a meaningful contribution to achieving the group's goals. Nevertheless, in order to maintain an enduring willingness of participation, stakeholders must develop a

DOI: 10.1057/9781137440006.0008

sense of belonging to the group. Especially interactions with other supporters and expressing endorsement for the group online are considered as involving digital practices. Overall, the Internet has the potential to assist groups in creating communities of committed citizens.

Note

1 The questions were part of the online survey that I had described in more detail in Chapter 2.

DOI: 10.1057/9781137440006.0008

5

How the Internet Shapes Collective Actions in the Future

Abstract: *To conclude the book, I will summarize in the final chapter the key messages and provide an outlook for questions and challenges that ought to be addressed in the future. I discuss the emergence of hybrid action networks, in which formal groups encourage personalized actions to attract previously unengaged individuals for their cause. Moreover, I highlight that the facilitating function of the Internet is restricted by the rate of adoption; especially effects of interactive practices are qualified as only a small proportion of users contribute content online. As a last point, I elaborate on the notion of surveillance and anonymity and speculate whether – as users are more inclined to navigate the Internet anonymously – Internet use continues to amplify mobilizing processes.*

Schumann, Sandy. *How the Internet Shapes Collective Actions.* Basingstoke: Palgrave Macmillan, 2015. DOI: 10.1057/9781137440006.0009.

DOI: 10.1057/9781137440006.0009

In an interview with the BBC Two series *The Virtual Revolution*, Stephen Fry describes the Internet as a radical innovation, "a great new world (....) [and] the most fantastic (...) development since Gutenberg produced his Bible" (2009, cited in: Krotoski, 2013, p. 145). Just like him, many consider the Internet as globe-shifting, revolutionizing even such complex social phenomena as collective actions (Van Dijk, 2012). And although a technology-deterministic perspective is certainly too restrictive (Morozov, 2011), anecdotal accounts as well as empirical evidence suggest that the Internet can shape the nature and enhance the scale of collective actions. In the following, I will summarize the previous chapters and discuss the challenges of an ever-growing line of research that examines the facilitating effects and dynamics of Internet use. Finally, I speculate about current technological developments and their influence on the future (de)mobilizing potential of the Internet.

Conclusion

Reports of past social movements and almost two decades of interdisciplinary research suggest that the use of social media platforms, services of computer-mediated communication, and websites can impact collective actions in three distinct ways. First of all, the participatory Internet affords self-organized forms of engagement that are not defined by the agenda of a formal group but by individual action frames. Social media platforms provide easy access to crucial information, offer a context to encounter like-minded citizens, and grant the space to deliberate on and coordinate collective actions in a decentralized manner. The connective actions (Bennett & Segerberg, 2012, 2013) emerge based on unique needs and aspirations; nevertheless, on a higher level, they still address collective concerns and strive for solutions to a collective problem. The motives, means, and methods to achieve these solutions, however, are not set in stone and can vary widely between supporters. Ultimately, the participatory Internet helps prompt a shift from group-brokered to crowd-enabled collective actions – a shift in the nature of collective actions. Consequently, collective actions are also becoming more inclusive, that is, they encourage participation of those who would not want to commit to the interpretations of a formal group and who would traditionally not be the target of organizational outreach efforts.

DOI: 10.1057/9781137440006.0009

Previous research further highlighted that using Internet-enabled technologies to acquire information and interact with fellow citizens can incite offline engagement, mediated by intrapersonal and intragroup mobilizing processes. For instance, quick and easy access to practical information about collective actions reduces the costs of participation and could foster attendance at protests or sit-ins. Gathering political news on the Internet increases voter turnout in particular for previously uninvolved citizens. Online discussions can strengthen identification with a group – a well-established predictor of collective actions (Van Zomeren et al., 2008). In addition, if digital dialogue is used to involve third parties – politicians, civil society, and citizens – in a group's struggle, collective identities are likely to be politicized and ultimately drive collective actions.

Finally, the Internet constitutes a platform for online collective actions that are independent of time, space, and the co-presence of fellow supporters. Websites that host tools for instrumental actions – for example, donations – and platforms that include features to voice and signal endorsement enable individuals to diversify their repertoire of contentions and allow involvement even when supporters do not have the resources to join collective actions offline. Citizens who were not yet engaged for a cause can turn to these digital tactics to take first steps towards enduring participation; many online collective actions are rather quick and easy and could constitute an initial rung on a ladder of engagement. Advocates of the slacktivism critique (Gladwell, 2010; Morozov, 2009) counter the latter argument and suggest that the low-cost and low-risk clicks and "likes" do in fact derail subsequent collective actions. My research pointed out that this substitute hypothesis can be endorsed, provided that supporters consider the low-threshold online collective actions as a substantial contribution to their group's success and welfare (Schumann & Klein, in press).

Keeping the aforementioned insights in mind, I completed my inquiry into *How the Internet Shapes Collective Actions* by reviewing the digital practices of cause-related, advocacy, and social movement organizations. To date, they primarily use the Internet to share information in a top-down process. As social media platforms are adopted at a growing rate, the groups might change this pattern and promote also interactions – with and between citizens – as well as the personalization of collective actions. After all, and as indicated in a study with Greenpeace supporters, gathering information online may be viewed as influential,

DOI: 10.1057/9781137440006.0009

but online deliberations and sharing material with one's personal social network are activities that provide a sense of involvement, possibly encouraging lasting commitment to the group.

Outlook

Since the uprising in the Arab world and the spread of the Occupy movement in 2011, scholars investigated increasingly the role of the Internet for collective actions. This work contributed important insights to theoretical and applied discourses. Nevertheless, the current literature also highlights a number of challenges. For instance, the strong distinction between organization-brokered and crowd-enabled collective actions that I drew in Chapter 1 dismisses the possibility of mixed or hybrid action networks (Bennett & Segerberg, 2012). Cause-related, advocacy, and social movement organizations rely on organizational growth to accomplish their goals. As noted by Cristancho and Anduiza (2013), when given the opportunity to follow individual action frames, otherwise unengaged citizens are likely to join protests to promote a collective goal – despite not identifying with and following the interpretations of a formal group. Grass-root organizations can tap into this potential by allowing supporters to personalize their engagement, providing looser modes of attachment and more flexible patterns of participation. Bennett and Segerberg (2012) described how such hybrid networks might be expressed in practice by referring to the Occupy movement: The General Assemblies that were held at Occupy protest sites around the world were central to assigning tasks, allocating resources, and coordinating actions. At the same time, social media platforms allowed those who did not want or who could not commit to this formal gathering to be involved, contribute their ideas, make donations, and mobilize more supporters. "Thus, even as *occupy* displayed some organizational development, it was defined by its self-organizing roots" (Bennett & Segerberg, 2012, p. 757).

In Chapter 2, I highlighted that low-cost and low-risk online collective actions are valid tactics in individuals' repertoires of contention, namely, because the latter are considered as a substantial contribution to attaining a group goal. What remains to be explored though is whether this expectation is indeed justified. Can Internet-based collective actions – signing petitions, sharing calls for actions, or expressing support symbolically through "likes" – truly advance a campaign? The digital actions may be rather short lived; they can attract quickly a lot of attention, but disappear from people's radar just as fast. For instance, it has been demonstrated that online petitions – if they gather at all a significant number of signatures – are most likely to be signed just after its launch; then the outreach drops within a few hours (Yasseri, Hale, & Margetts, 2013).

Future research is necessary to support the causal impact of online collective actions. First evidence pointed out that the latter relate to individuals' subsequent action tendencies (Kristofferson et al., 2014; Schumann & Klein, in press). It has, however, not been established whether digital tactics of contention also impact the success of concrete initiatives or policy processes. To what extent are politicians taking online petitions and Facebook "likes" into account when they decide on new laws and regulations? And is it more likely that grass-root organizations implement community programs if they receive ample endorsement online?

On a more general note, scholars need to acknowledge explicitly that the Internet shapes collective actions only to the extent that citizens and civil society have access to, know how to use, and have time to spend on the Internet. Even though the rate of Internet adoption is growing at a staggering rate, the majority of people around the globe are not (yet) visiting social media platforms, services of CMC, and websites with the same frequency as, for instance, citizens of many Western countries. The potential of the Internet to foster collective actions in these contexts is reduced. In fact, it has been criticized that during the uprisings in Egypt in 2011, the impact of social media platforms was overestimated. Only roughly one third of Egyptian households had access to the Internet (Ahram, 2013) and interpersonal, face-to-face communication still played a central role for facilitating participation in the protests (Tufekci & Wilson, 2012).

Moreover, the impact of the participatory Internet on collective actions is restricted in the sense that most Internet users are only gathering but not contributing content online. Ben McConnell (2006) suggested that only 1 per cent of users of a particular Internet community are actively generating content, while the remaining 99 per cent are lurking. On the bright side, the mobilizing potential of information appears to be large. On the other hand, although empirical evidence suggests that online discussions may promote engagement, the influence of this digital practice is certainly less pronounced if users are not joining the dialogue.

DOI: 10.1057/9781137440006.0009

To conclude the outlook, I want to explore two technological developments that may influence how the Internet shapes collective actions in the future. Government agencies, technology enterprises as well as cause-related, advocacy, and social movement organizations are increasingly applying sophisticated tools to trace and analyse users' every step online; they are even able to reverse engineer users' gender, age, and post-code (Tufekci, 2014b). This trend is worthy to discuss from (at least) two angles: Users' (lack of) anonymity and the personalization or algorithmic filtering of information.

Google announced in the summer of 2014 that when registering with its services, users are no longer required to report their real name. The Tor Project strives to create a possibility to access the Internet without leaving digital footprints or giving away users' physical location. At the moment, it seems as if "offers" to access the Internet while remaining anonymous are only interesting for a small number of Internet users. Individuals are concerned about privacy. Nevertheless, they share insights about their everyday life publicly online – a phenomenon that is referred to as the privacy paradox (Barnes, 2006). For instance, if citizens know that social media platforms technically afford the control of personal information, privacy concerns are reduced, and users are more likely to post sensitive information (Brandimarte, Acquisti, & Loewenstein, 2013).

It could be speculated that these patterns change, as Internet use skills develop, as large scale privacy infringements are repeatedly discussed in the public discourse, and as the services that grant anonymity receive more attention. In that case, will the Internet continue to shape collective actions? First the unprecedented access to information is likely facilitating participation in collective actions regardless of users' anonymity. In addition, a review of the security practices on Jihadi web forums indicated that tools for encryption and anonymous Internet use might actually serve an identity-construing function (grugq, 2014): By using, for example, Tor to access the Internet, individuals suggested that they belong to the group of Jihadis.

Moreover, the SIDE model (Spears et al., 1990) highlights that interactions amongst anonymous group members enhance the influence of group norms, increase group identification, and the polarization of attitudes in line with group norms. Concluding, cause-related, advocacy, and social movement organizations may benefit from allowing supporters to choose whether they want to share personal information. Remaining anonymous when engaging in discussions or when sharing

DOI: 10.1057/9781137440006.0009

content online may serve the individual user to protect its privacy and serve groups as it strengthens members' sense of belonging.

One goal of the efforts to track users' every click and "like" is to develop targeted marketing or political campaigning. Zeynep Tufekci (2014b) highlighted that such computational politics foster "public's unease with algorithmic manipulation (....) because it is opaque, powerful and possibly non-consensual (...) in an environment of information asymmetry" (para. 70). Moreover, as information promotes action, algorithmic filtering can impact citizens' engagement in protests, sit-ins, or campaigns. The severity of algorithmic filtering became evident during the demonstrations in Ferguson (USA) in the summer of 2014. After the black teenager Michael Brown was shot by a police officer on 9 August, citizens of the town of Ferguson protested against the killing. Cable-news did not report about the shooting until two days after; on Twitter already on 9 August 146,183 tweets were posted (Zuckerman, 2014). The issue attention on Twitter and Facebook – both being popular social media platforms – was, however, not the same (see also Tufekci, 2014a).

Interestingly, compared to another viral campaign – the ALS Ice Bucket Challenge – about eight times as many posts were published about Ferguson on Facebook. But Facebook users were not exposed to eight times more stories about Ferguson. It seems as if Facebook's algorithm pushed posts about the Ice Bucket Challenge more than updates about Ferguson. After all, Facebook aims to inform users about material that keeps them in a positive mood; controversial topics such as race and class are less likely to be promoted (Zuckerman, 2014). Consequently, however, less citizens learn about pressing social issues, become interested in, and ready to act for (or against) the struggles of a disadvantaged group. And ultimately, the Internet is losing its potential to shape collective actions.

DOI: 10.1057/9781137440006.0009

Bibliography

Ahram (2013). Egypt internet users reached 36 million in June 2013: MCIT. Retrieved from http://english.ahram.org.eg/NewsContent/3/12/84996/Business/Economy/Egypt internet-users-reached--million-in-June--MCI.aspx

Alberici, A. I., & Milesi, P. (2013). The influence of the internet on the psychosocial predictors of collective action. *Journal of Community and Applied Social Psychology, 23,* 373–388.

Anduiza, E., Cristancho, C., & Sabucedo, J. M. (2014). Mobilization through online social networks: The political protest of the Indignados in Spain. *Information, Communication & Society, 17,* 750–764.

Arnstein, S. R. (1969). A ladder of citizen participation. *Journal of the American Institute of Planners, 35,* 216–224.

Bakshy, E. (2012). Rethinking information diversity in networks. Retrieved from https://www.facebook.com/notes/facebook-data-team/rethinking-information-diversity-in-networks/10150503499618859

Baumgartner, J. C., & Morris, J. S. (2010). Who wants to be my friend? Obama, youth and social networks in the 2008 campaign. *Communicator-In-Chief: How Barack Obama used new media technology to win the White House,* 51–66.

Barnes, S. B. (2006). A privacy paradox: Social networking in the United States. *First Monday, 11.* Retrieved from http://firstmonday.org/article/view/1394/1312

Bennett, W. L., & Segerberg, A. (2012). The logic of connective action: Digital media and the personalization of contentious politics. *Information, Communication & Society, 15*, 739–768.

Bennett, W. L., & Segerberg, A. (2013). *The logic of connective action: Digital media and the personalization of contentious politics.* Cambridge, UK: Cambridge University Press.

Bimber, B. (2003). *Information and American democracy: Technology in the evolution of political power.* Cambridge, UK: Cambridge University Press.

Bimber, B., Cunill, M. C., Copeland, L., & Gibson, R. (2014). Digital media and political participation the moderating role of political interest across acts and over time. *Social Science Computer Review*, published before print.

Bimber, B., Flanagin, A., & Stohl, C. (2012). *Collective action in organizations: Interaction and engagement in an era of technological change.* Cambridge, UK: Cambridge University Press.

Bliuc, A. M., McGarty, C., Reynolds, K., & Muntele, D. (2007). Opinion-based group membership as a predictor of commitment to political action. *European Journal of Social Psychology, 37*, 19–32.

Bond, R. M., Fariss, C. J., Jones, J. J., Kramer, A. D., Marlow, C., Settle, J. E., & Fowler, J. H. (2012). A 61-million-person experiment in social influence and political mobilization. *Nature, 489*, 295–298.

Boulianne, S. (2009). Does internet use affect engagement? A meta-analysis research. *Political Communication, 26*, 193–211.

Boulianne, S. (2011). Stimulating or reinforcing political interest: Using panel data to examine reciprocal effects between news media and political interest. *Political Communication, 28*, 147–162.

Bortree, D. S., & Seltzer, T. (2009). Dialogic strategies and outcomes: An analysis of environmental advocacy groups' Facebook profiles. *Public Relations Review, 35*, 317–319.

Brandimarte, L., Acquisti, A., & Loewenstein, G. (2013). Misplaced confidences privacy and the control paradox. *Social Psychological and Personality Science, 4*, 340–347.

Briones, R. L., Kuch, B., Liu, B. F., & Jin, Y. (2011). Keeping up with the digital age: How the American Red Cross uses social media to build relationships. *Public Relations Review, 37*, 37–43.

Brunsting, S., & Postmes, T. (2002). Social movement participation in the digital age predicting offline and online collective action. *Small Group Research, 33*, 525–554.

DOI: 10.1057/9781137440006.0010

Byrne, D., & Clore, G. L. (1970). A reinforcement model of evaluation processes. *Personality: An International Journal, 1*, 103–123.

Calderaro, A., & Kavada, A. (2013). Special issue on "Online Collective Action and Policy Change". *Policy & Internet, 5*, 1–6.

Carroll, R. (2012, 21 April). Kony 2012 Cover the Night fails to move from the internet to the streets. *The Guardian*. Retrieved from http://www.theguardian.com/world/2012/apr/21/kony-2012-campaign-uganda-warlord

Castano, E., Yzerbyt, V., Paladino, M. P., & Sacchi, S. (2002). I belong, therefore, I exist: Ingroup identification, ingroup entitativity, and ingroup bias. *Personality and Social Psychology Bulletin, 28*, 135–143.

Christensen, H. (2011). Political activities on the internet: Slacktivism or political participation by other means? *First Monday, 2*. Retrieved from http://firstmonday.org/ojs/index.php/fm/article/viewArticle/3336

Condon, J. W., & Crano, W. D. (1988). Inferred evaluation and the relation between attitude similarity and interpersonal attraction. *Journal of Personality and Social Psychology, 54*, 789–797.

Cristancho, C., & Anduiza, E. (2013, March). Connective action in European mass protest. Paper presented at the Joint Sessions of the European Consortium for Political Science Research-Online Collective Action Workshop, Mainz, Germany.

Diamond, L. (2010). Liberation technology. *Journal of Democracy, 21*, 69–83.

Döring, N. (2010). *Sozialpsychologie des Internets [Social psychology of the internet]*. Göttingen, Germany: Hogrefe.

Earl, J. (2010). The dynamics of protest-related diffusion on the web. *Information, Communication & Society, 13*, 209–225.

Eissenstat, H. (2014, 16 April). How much do you know about Turkey's Twitter ban? [Web log post]. Retrieved from http://blog.amnestyusa.org/europe/how-much-do-you-know- about-turkeys-twitter-trial/

Elazari, K. (March 2014). Hackers: The internet's immune system [video]. Retrieved from http://www.ted.com/talks/keren_elazari_hackers_the_internet_s_immune_system

Emmer, M., Vowe, G., & Wolling, J. (2011). *Bürger online. Die Entwicklung der politischen Online-Kommunikation in Deutschland [The development of political online communication in Germany]*. Konstanz, Germany: UVK.

DOI: 10.1057/9781137440006.0010

Eurostat (2014). Internet activities – individuals [Database]. Retrieved from http://appsso.eurostat.ec.europa.eu/nui/show. do?dataset=isoc_ci_ac_i&lang=en

Eveland Jr, W. P., Hayes, A. F., Shah, D. V., & Kwak, N. (2005). Understanding the relationship between communication and political knowledge: A model comparison approach using panel data. *Political Communication, 22,* 423–446.

Eveland, W. P., & Hively, M. H. (2009). Political discussion frequency, network size, and "heterogeneity" of discussion as predictors of political knowledge and participation. *Journal of Communication, 59,* 205–224.

Eveland, W. P., Shah, D. V., & Kwak, N. (2003). Assessing causality in the cognitive mediation model panel study of motivations, information processing, and learning during Campaign 2000. *Communication Research, 30,* 359–386.

Festinger, L. (1957). *A theory of cognitive dissonance.* Evanston, IL: Row, Peterson.

Fisher, D. R., & Boekkooi, M. (2010). Mobilizing friends and strangers: Understanding the role of the internet in the step it up day of action. *Information, Communication & Society, 13,* 193–208.

Fishbach, A., Henderson, M. D., & Koo, M. (2011). Pursuing goals with others: Group identification and motivation resulting from things done versus things left undone. *Journal of Experimental Psychology: General, 140,* 520–534.

Flanagin, A. J., Stohl, C., & Bimber, B. (2006). Modeling the structure of collective action. *Communication Monographs, 73,* 29–54.

Freelon, D. (2014). Online civic activism: Where does it fit? *Policy & Internet, 6,* 192–198.

Gardner, A. (2014, 16 April). Turkey Twitter trial [Web log post]. Retrieved from http://livewire.amnesty.org/2014/04/16/turkey-twitter-trial/

Gil de Zúñiga, H., Jung, N., & Valenzuela, S. (2012). Social media use for news and individuals' social capital, civic engagement and political participation. *Journal of Computer-Mediated Communication, 17,* 319–336.

Gil de Zúñiga, H. G., & Valenzuela, S. (2011). The mediating path to a stronger citizenship: Online and offline networks, weak ties, and civic engagement. *Communication Research, 38,* 397–421.

Gil de Zúñiga, H., Veenstra, A., Vraga, E., & Shah, D. (2010). Digital democracy: Reimagining pathways to political participation. *Journal of Information Technology & Politics, 7,* 36–51.

DOI: 10.1057/9781137440006.0010

Gladwell, M. (2010, 4 October). Small change. Why the revolution will not be tweeted. *The New Yorker.* Retrieved from http://www.newyorker.com/reporting/2010/10/04/101004fa_fact_gladwell

Göle, N. (2013, 2 June). Anatomy of public square movement. *Todays Zaman.* Retrieved from http://www.todayszaman.com/news-317643-gezi-anatomy-of-public-square- movementby-nilufer-gole-.html

González-Bailón, S., Borge-Holthoefer, J., & Moreno, Y. (2013). Broadcasters and hidden influentials in online protest diffusion. *American Behavioral Scientist.* Retrieved from http://arxiv.org/pdf/1203.1868.pdf

Gordon, E., Baldwin-Philippi, J., & Balestra, M. (2013). Why we engage: How theories of human behavior contribute to our understanding of civic engagement in a digital era. *The Social Science Research Network Electronic Paper Collection.* Retrieved from hhtp://ssrn.com/abstract=2343762

Graham, M., & De Sabbata, S. (2013). Internet population and penetration [Map]. Retrieved from http://geography.oii.ox.ac.uk/?page=internet-population-and-penetration

Granovetter, M. S. (1973). The strength of weak ties. *American Journal of Sociology, 78,* 1360–1380.

grugq (2014, 9 August). Jihadist fan club cryptoCrap [Web log post]. Retrieved from http://grugq.github.io/blog/2014/08/09/jihadist-fan-crypto/

Guéguen, N., & Jacob, C. (2002). Social presence reinforcement and computer-mediated communication: The effect of the solicitor's photography on compliance to a survey request made by e-mail. *Cyber Psychology & Behavior, 5,* 139–142.

Guo, C., & Saxton, G. D. (2014). Tweeting social change: How social media are changing nonprofit advocacy. *Nonprofit and Voluntary Sector Quarterly, 43,* 57–79.

Harlow, S., & Guo, L. (2014). Will the revolution be tweeted or facebooked? Using digital communication tools in immigrant activism. *Journal of Computer-Mediated Communication, 19,* 463–478.

Hutchinson, S. (2013, 4 June). Social media plays major part in Turkey protests. *BBC.* Retrieved from http://www.bbc.com/news/world-europe-22772352

Internet Live Stats (2014a). Number of internet users. Retrieved from http://www.internetlivestats.com/internet-users/

DOI: 10.1057/9781137440006.0010

Internet Live Stats (2014b). Total number of websites. Retrieved from http:// www.internetlivestats.com/total-number-of-websites/

Invisible Children (2014). Year in review: Results. Retrieved from http://invisiblechildren.com/kony/

Kaplan, A. M., & Haenlein, M. (2010). Users of the world, unite! The challenges and opportunities of social media. *Business Horizons, 53,* 59–68.

Karpf, D. (2010). Online political mobilization from the advocacy group's perspective: Looking beyond clicktivism. *Policy & Internet, 2,* 7–41.

Katz, E., Blumler, J. G., & Gurevitch, M. (1974). *The uses and gratifications approach to mass communication.* Beverly Hills, CA: Sage.

Kavada, A. (2012). Engagement, bonding and identity across multiple platforms: Avaaz on Facebook, YouTube, and MySpace. *MedieKultur* 52: 28–48.

Khazan, O. (April 30, 2013). UNICEF Tells Slacktivists: Give Money, Not Facebook Likes. *The Atlantic.* Retrieved from http://www.theatlantic. com/international/archive/2013/04/unicef-tells-slacktivists-give-money-not-facebook-likes/275429/

Kim, Y., & Yoo, J. J. S. (2014). The public as active agents in social movement: Facebook and Gangjeong movement. *Computers in Human Behavior, 37,* 144–151.

Klandermans, B. (1997). *The social psychology of protest.* Oxford, UK: Basil Blackwell.

Klein, O., Spears, R., & Reicher, S. (2007). Social identity performance: Extending the Strategic side of SIDE. *Personality and Social Psychology Review, 1,* 1–18.

Knobloch-Westerwick, S., & Johnson, B. K. (2014). Selective exposure for better or worse: Its mediating role for online news' impact on political participation. *Journal of Computer-Mediated Communication, 19,* 184–196.

Kraut, R., Patterson, M., Lundmark, V., Kiesler, S., Mukophadhyay, T., & Scherlis, W. (1998). Internet paradox: A social technology that reduces social involvement and psychological well-being? *American Psychologist, 53,* 1017–1031.

Kraut, R., Kiesler, S., Boneva, B., Cummings, J., Helgeson, V., & Crawford, A. (2002). Internet paradox revisited. *Journal of Social Issues, 58,* 49–74.

Kristofferson, K., White, K., & Peloza, J. (2013). The nature of slacktivism: How the social observability of an initial act of token

DOI: 10.1057/9781137440006.0010

support affects subsequent prosocial action. *Journal of Consumer Research*. Advance online publication. Retrieved from http://web.missouri.edu/~segerti/capstone/Slacktivism.pdf

Krotoski, A. (2013). *Untangling the web*. London, UK: Faber & Faber.

Kruikemeier, S., van Noort, G., Vliegenthart, R., & de Vreese, C. H. (2013). Unraveling the effects of active and passive forms of political Internet use: Does it affect citizens' political involvement? *New Media & Society*, published online first.

Lea, M., Spears, R., & de Groot, D. (2001). Knowing me, knowing you: Anonymity effects on social identity processes within groups. *Personality and Social Psychology Bulletin, 27*, 526–537.

Lazarsfeld, P., & Merton, R. K. (1954). Friendship as a social process: A substantive and Methodological analysis. In M. Berger, T. Abel, & C. H. Page (Eds.), *Freedom and control in modern society* (pp. 18–66). New York: Van Nostrand.

Lee, Y. H., & Hsieh, G. (2013). Does slacktivism hurt activism?: The effects of moral balancing and consistency in online activism. In W. E. Mackay, S. Brewster, & S. Bodker (Eds.), *Proceedings of the SIGCHI Conference on Human Factors in Computing Systems* (pp. 811–820). New York : ACM. Retrieved from http://faculty.washington.edu/garyhs/docs/lee-chi2013-slacktivism.pdf

Leonard, C. (2009, 1 September). In defense of "slacktivism" [Web log post]. Retrieved from http://bayercenter.wordpress.com/2009/09/01/in-defense-of-slacktivism/

Letsch, C. (2013, 3 June). Social media and opposition to blame for protests, says Turkish PM. *The Guardian*. Retrieved from http://www.guardian.co.uk/world/2013/jun/02/turkish-protesters

Lim, M. (2013). Many clicks but little sticks: Social media activism in Indonesia. *Journal of Contemporary Asia, 43*, 636–657.

Loader, B. D., & Mercea, D. (2011). Networking democracy? Social media innovations and participatory politics. *Information, Communication & Society, 14*, 757–769.

Lotan, G., Graeff, E., Ananny, M., Gaffney, D., & Pearce, I. (2011). The Arab Spring the revolutions were tweeted: Information flows during the 2011 Tunisian and Egyptian revolutions. *International Journal of Communication, 5*, 1375–1405.

Lovejoy, K., & Saxton, G. D. (2012). Information, community, and action: How nonprofit organizations use social media. *Journal of Computer-Mediated Communication, 17*, 337–353.

DOI: 10.1057/9781137440006.0010

Macafee, T., & De Simone, J. J. (2012). Killing the bill online? Pathways to young people's protest engagement via social media. *Cyberpsychology, Behavior, and Social Networking, 15,* 579- 584.

Margetts, H., John, P., Escher, T., & Reissfelder, S. (2011). Social information and political participation on the internet: An experiment. *European Political Science Review, 3,* 321–344.

Martin, J., Brickman, P., & Murray, A. (1984). Moral outrage and pragmatism: Explanations for collective action. *Journal of Experimental Social Psychology, 20,* 484–496.

McConnell, B. (2006, 3 May). The 1% rule: Charting citizen participation [Web log post] Retrieved from http://web.archive. org/web/20100511081141/http://www.churchofthecustomer.com/ blog/2006/05/charting_wiki_p.html

Melucci, A. (1996). *Challenging codes: Collective action in the information age.* Cambridge, UK: Cambridge University Press.

Morozov, E. (2009, 19 May). The brave new world of slacktivism [Web log post]. Retrieved from http://neteffect.foreignpolicy.com/posts/2009/05/19/ the_brave_new_world_of_slacktivism

Morozov, E. (2011, 7 March). Facebook and Twitter are just places revolutionaries go. *The Guardian.* Retrieved from http://www. theguardian.com/commentisfree/2011/mar/07/facebook- twitter- revolutionaries-cyber-utopians

Nah, S., Veenstra, A. S., & Shah, D. V. (2006). The internet and anti-war activism: A case study of information, expression, and action. *Journal of Computer-Mediated Communication, 12,* 230–247.

Obar, J. A., Zube, P., & Lampe, C. (2012). Advocacy 2.0: An analysis of how advocacy groups in the United States perceive and use social media as tools for facilitating civic engagement and collective action. *Journal of Information Policy, 2.* Retrieved from http://jip.vmhost.psu. edu/ojs/index.php/jip/article/view/80/47

Olson, M. (1968). *The logic of collective action: Public goods and the theory of groups.* New York: Schocken Books.

Postmes, T., & Brunsting, S. (2002). Collective action in the age of the internet mass Communication and online mobilization. *Social Science Computer Review, 20,* 290–301.

Postmes, T., Haslam, S. A., & Swaab, R. I. (2005). Social influence in small groups: An interactive model of social identity formation. *European Review of Social Psychology, 16,* 1–42.

DOI: 10.1057/9781137440006.0010

Postmes, T., Spears, R., Lee, A. T., & Novak, R. J. (2005). Individuality and social influence in groups: Inductive and deductive routes to group identity. *Journal of Personality and Social Psychology, 89,* 747–763.

Postmes, T., Spears, R., Sakhel, K., & De Groot, D. (2001). Social influence in computer- mediated communication: The effects of anonymity on group behavior. *Personality and Social Psychology Bulletin, 27,* 1243–1254.

Putnam, R. D. (1995). Bowling alone: America's declining social capital. *Journal of Democracy, 6,* 65–78.

Rainie, L., Purcell, K., & Smith, A. (2011). *The social side of the internet.* Washington, D.C. : Pew Internet and American Life Project.

Roggenband, C., & Klandermans, B. (2010). Introduction. In B. Klandermans & C. Roggeband (Eds.), *Handbook of social movements across disciplines* (pp. 1–12). New York: Springer.

Ronfeldt, D., Arquilla, J., Fuller, G. F., & Fuller, M. (1998). The Zapatista social netwar in Mexico. Santa Monica: RAND.

Rudolph, U. (2009). *Motivations psychology Kompakt. [Motivation psychology compact].* Weinheim, Germany: Beltz.

Sassenberg, K., & Boos, M. (2003). Attitude change in computer-mediated communication: Effects of anonymity and category norms. *Group Processes & Intergroup Relations, 6,* 405–422.

Scheufele, D. A., & Tewksbury, D. (2007). Framing, agenda setting, and priming: The evolution of three media effects models. *Journal of Communication, 57,* 9–20.

Schumann, S., & Klein, O. (in press). Substitute or stepping stone? Assessing the impact of low-threshold online collective actions on offline participation. *European Journal of Social Psychology.*

Seo, H., Kim, J. Y., & Yang, S. U. (2009). Global activism and new media: A study of transnational NGOs' online public relations. *Public Relations Review, 35,* 123–126.

Shah, D. V., Cho, J., Eveland, W. P., & Kwak, N. (2005). Information and expression in a digital age modeling Internet effects on civic participation. *Communication Research, 32,* 531–565.

Shah, D. V., Kwak, N., & Holbert, R. L. (2001). "Connecting" and "disconnecting" with civic life: Patterns of Internet use and the production of social capital. *Political Communication, 18,* 141–162.

Simon, B., & Klandermans, B. (2001). Politicized collective identity: A social psychological analysis. *American Psychologist, 56,* 319.

DOI: 10.1057/9781137440006.0010

Skinner, J. (2011). Social media and revolution: The Arab Spring and the Occupy Movement as seen through three information studies paradigms. *Sprouts: Working Papers on Information Systems, 11.*Retrieved from http://sprouts.aisnet.org/11–169.

Smith, J., & Fetner, T. (2010). Structural approaches in the sociology of social movements. In B. Klandermans & C. Roggeband (Eds.), *Handbook of Social Movements Across Disciplines* (pp. 13–57). New York: Springer.

Smith, A., & Rainie, L. (2010). 8% of online Americans use Twitter. Retrieved from http://www.pewinternet.org/2010/12/09/8-of-online-americans-use-twitter/

Sotirovic, M., & McLeod, J. M. (2001). Values, communication behavior, and political participation. *Political Communication, 18,* 273–300.

Spears, R., & Lea, M. (1994). Panacea or panopticon? The hidden power in computer-mediated communication. *Communication Research, 21,* 427–459.

Spears, R., Lea, M., & Lee, S. (1990). De-individuation and group polarization in computer-mediated communication. *British Journal of Social Psychology, 29,* 121–134.

Spears, R., Postmes, T., Lea, M., & Wolbert, A. (2002). When are net effects gross products? *Journal of Social Issues, 58,* 91–107.

Stürmer, S., & Simon, B. (2004). The role of collective identification in social movement participation: A panel study in the context of the German gay movement. *Personality and Social Psychology Bulletin, 30,* 263–277.

Stürmer, S., Simon, B., Loewy, M., & Jörger, H. (2003). The dual-pathway model of social movement participation: The case of the fat acceptance movement. *Social Psychology Quarterly, 66,* 71–82.

Sunstein, C. (2002). The law of group polarization. *The Journal of Political Philosophy, 10,* 175–195.

Tajfel, H. (1972). Social categorization (La Categorisation Sociale). In S. Moscovici (Ed.), *Introduction a La Psychologie Sociale Vol. 1* (pp. 272–302). Paris, France: Larousse.

Tajfel, H. & Turner, J. C. (1979). An integrative theory of inter-group conflict. In W. G. Austin & S. Worchel (Eds.), *The social psychology of intergroup relations* (pp. 33–47). Monterey: Brooks/Cole.

Taylor, J. R., & Van Every, E. J. (2000). *The emergent organization: Communication as its site and surface.* Mahwah, New Jersey and London: Lawrence Erlbaum Associates.

DOI: 10.1057/9781137440006.0010

Theocharis, Y., Lowe, W., van Deth, J. W., & Albacete, G. M. G. (2013). Using Twitter to mobilise protest action: Transnational online mobilisation patterns and action repertoires in the occupy Wall Street, Indignados and Aganaktismenoi movements. Retrieved from http://dl.conjugateprior.org/preprints/ecprjs-theocharis-et-al.pdf

Tropp, L., & Brown, A. (2004). What benefits the group can also benefit the individual: Group-enhancing and individual-enhancing motives for collective actions. Group Processes & Intergroup Relations, 7, 267–282.

Tufekci, Z. (2012, 10 March). #Kony2012, Understanding networked symbolic action & Why slacktivism is conceptually misleading [Web log post]. Retrieved from http://technosociology.org/?p=904

Tufekci, Z. (2014a). Big data, surveillance and computational politics. First Monday, 19. Retrieved from http://firstmonday.org/ojs/index. php/fm/article/view/4901/4097

Tufekci Z. (2014b, 14 August). What happens to #Ferguson affects Ferguson: Net neutrality, algorithmic filtering and Ferguson [Web log post]. Retrieved from https://medium.com/message/ferguson-is-also-a-net-neutrality-issue-6d2f3db51eb0

Tufekci, Z., & Freelon, D. (2013). Introduction to the special issue on new media and social unrest. American Behavioral Scientist, 57, 843–847.

Tufekci, Z., & Wilson, C. (2012). Social media and the decision to participate in political Protest: Observations from Tahir Square. Journal of Communication, 2, 363–379.

Turner, J. C. (1999). Some current issues in research on social identity and self-categorization theories. In N. Ellemers, R. Spears, & B. Doosje (Eds.), Social identity: Context, commitment, content (pp. 6–34). Oxford: Blackwell.

Turner, J. C., Hogg, M. A., Oakes, P. J., Reicher, S. D., & Wetherell, M. S. (1987). Rediscovering the social group. A self-categorization theory. Oxford: Blackwell.

Valenzuela, S., Arriagada, A., & Scherman, A. (2012). The social media basis of youth protest behavior: The case of Chile. Journal of Communication, 62, 299–314.

Van Dijk, J. (2012). The network society. London: Sage Publications.

Van Laer, J., & Van Aelst, P. (2010). Cyber-protest and civil society: The Internet and action repertoires in social movements. In Y. Jewkes and

DOI: 10.1057/9781137440006.0010

M. Yar (Eds.), *Handbook of Internet crime* (pp. 230–254). Cullompton, UK: Willan Publishing.

Van Zomeren, M., & Iyer, A. (2009). Introduction to the social and psychological dynamics of collective action. *Journal of Social Issues, 65,* 645–660.

Van Zomeren, M., Postmes, T., & Spears, R. (2008). Toward an integrative social identity model of collective action: A quantitative research synthesis of three socio-psychological perspectives. *Psychological Bulletin, 134,* 504–535.

Van Zomeren, M., Postmes, T., & Spears, R. (2012). On conviction's collective consequences: Integrating moral conviction with the social identity model of collective action. *British Journal of Social Psychology, 51,* 52–71.

Varol, O., Ferrara, E., Ogan, C. L., Menczer, F., & Flammini, A. (2014). Evolution of online user behavior during a social upheaval. In *Proceedings of the 2014 ACM conference on Web science* (pp. 81–90). ACM.

Vasi, I. B., & Suh, C. S. (2013). Protest in the internet age: Public attention, social media, and the spread of 'Occupy' protests in the United States. Retrieved from http://politicsandprotest.ws.gc.cuny.edu/files/2012/07/PPW-2-Vasi.pdf

Verba, S., Schlozman, K. L., & Brady, H. E. (1995). *Voice and equality: Civic voluntarism in American politics.* Massachusetts: Harvard University Press.

Vissers, S., & Stolle, D. (2012). Spill-over effects between Facebook and on/offline political participation? Evidence from a two-wave panel study. Retrieved from https://www.cpsa- acsp.ca/papers-2012/Vissers-Stolle.pdf

Vissers, S., Hooghe, M., Stolle, D., & Mahéo, V. A. (2011). The impact of mobilization media on off- line and online participation: Are mobilization effects medium- specific? *Social Science Computer Review,* Retrieved from https://lirias.kuleuven.be/bitstream/123456789/291685/1/Social+Science+Computer+Review+2011+proofs.pdf

Vitak, J., Zube, P., Smock, A., Carr, C. T., Ellison, N., & Lampe, C. (2011). It's complicated: Facebook users' political participation in the 2008 election. *CyberPsychology, Behavior, and Social Networking, 14,* 107–114. DOI: 10.1089/cyber.2009.0226

Waggener Edstrom Worldwide Inc. & Georgetown University (2013). *Digital persuasion: How social media motivates action and drives support*

for causes. Retrieved from http://waggeneredstrom.com/downloads/
DSCA-Summary.pdf

Waters, R. D., Burnett, E., Lamm, A., & Lucas, J. (2009). Engaging
stakeholders through social networking: How nonprofit
organizations are using Facebook. *Public Relations Review, 35,* 102–106.

Wright, S. C., Taylor, D. M., & Moghaddam, F. M. (1990). Responding to
membership in a disadvantaged group: From acceptance to collective
protest. *Journal of Personality and Social Psychology, 58,* 994–1003.

Xenos, M., & Moy, P. (2007). Direct and differential effects of the
internet on political and civic engagement. *Journal of Communication,
57,* 704–718.

Yasseri, T., Hale, S., & Margetts, H. (submitted). Modeling the Rise
in Internet-based Petitions. Retrieved from: http://arxiv.org/
pdf1308.0239v1.pdf.

Zuckerman, E. (2012, 13 March). Unpacking KONY 2012 [Web log post].
Retrieved from http://isnblog.ethz.ch/social-media/unpacking-
kony-2012

Zuckerman, E. (2014, 27 August). Self-segregation on social networks
and the implications for the Ferguson, MO story [Web log post].
Retrieved from http://www.ethanzuckerman.com/blog/2014/08/27/
self-segregation-on-social-networks-and-the-implications-for-the-
ferguson-mo-story/

DOI: 10.1057/9781137440006.0010

Index

DOI: 10.1057/9781137440006.0011